Charles Anderson Dana

Eastern journeys

some notes of travel in Russia, in the Caucasus, and to Jerusalem

Charles Anderson Dana

Eastern journeys
some notes of travel in Russia, in the Caucasus, and to Jerusalem

ISBN/EAN: 9783744745062

Printed in Europe, USA, Canada, Australia, Japan

Cover: Foto ©Andreas Hilbeck / pixelio.de

More available books at **www.hansebooks.com**

Eastern Journeys

SOME NOTES OF TRAVEL
IN RUSSIA, IN THE CAUCASUS,
AND TO JERUSALEM

BY

CHARLES A. DANA

NEW YORK
D. APPLETON AND COMPANY
1898

CONTENTS.

RUSSIA AND THE CAUCASUS.

		PAGE
I.	Across the Four Seas to Odessa	1
II.	The Russian Riviera	17
III.	The Southern Aspects of the Caucasus	34
IV.	Tiflis and Trans-Caucasia	45
V.	Through the Darial Pass to Rostov	62
VI.	Nijni, the New City	78
VII.	Moscow and Warsaw	87

JERUSALEM.

VIII.	How to get there	107
IX.	The Holy City	118
X.	Bethlehem and Bethany	138

EASTERN JOURNEYS.

I.

ACROSS THE FOUR SEAS TO ODESSA.

It was a beautiful afternoon in May when our ship steamed out of the harbor of Marseilles. We had laid out an interesting scheme of travel, and we were now beginning its realization. We were going through the Mediterranean, stopping at two places in Greece, thence to Salonica and Constantinople, and from there to Odessa in Russia. From there by ship the whole length of the Black Sea to Batoum, thence by rail to Tiflis and Baku on the Caspian Sea, then again by rail to Samarcand in Turkestan, and finally back from Central Asia through European Russia, Poland, and Germany to the Atlantic again, and so to New York, making in all from the commencement to the end a journey of perhaps sixteen thousand miles.

It began most pleasantly, and so it continued to the close. Not a single storm of any importance, not a mishap of any kind came to interfere with our comfort. It is true we were not able to get beyond the boundaries of trans-Caucasia; but that was due to the temporary breaking up of the mountain railway between Tiflis and Baku. Apart from that we were able to carry out our full plan, and in due time we found ourselves safely at home again on the delightful borders of Long Island Sound.

We had the luck to pass through the Strait of Bonifacio, which separates Corsica from Sardinia, in full daylight, so that we could see fairly the extreme points of each of these famous islands. They are hilly and wooded near the strait, and one could not help wishing to go ashore on each and explore the whole interior. Next day we passed among the Lipari Islands and saw both the crater of Etna and the smoking cone of Stromboli. The Strait of Messina, between Italy and Sicily, we reached just as the twilight was coming on, and the only idea we could gain of the scenery was from the vague outlines of the heights and the mass of twinkling lights in the streets and houses gleaming through the darkness and showing the position of Messina.

Charybdis and Scylla are passed almost without noticing either. Yet, we reflected, a whirlpool which could make a great disturbance and danger to navigation in the time of Ulysses might prove only a trifle to a modern steamer of six thousand tons.

The plan of our voyage included two landings in Greece, one at Kalamata in the ancient Peloponnesus, and the other at Syra, an island among the Cyclades.

We were very glad of this opportunity to see something more of the modern Greeks and of the cities they live in. Kalamata is at the head of the Gulf of Koron, some thirty or forty miles north of Cape Matapan. It is a busy, manufacturing, modern place of five thousand to eight thousand inhabitants. The principal industry appears to be the manufacture of silk. Our anchor was hardly thrown out before peddlers of silk things were on board, selling what they could to the passengers. The goods seemed to be hand-woven, solid and substantial, and of only two or three simple colors. Handkerchiefs worth from one to two francs each, and pretty scarfs, thin and gauzy, formed the principal articles of these dealers' traffic. They also had white and drab materials for women's dresses, but I saw no printed stuffs.

From Kalamata to Syra occupied a whole night, taking us around the southern extremity of Greece and to a considerable distance eastward from the coast. Syra, with its thirty thousand or forty thousand people, is a very attractive place, entirely European in appearance, with fine residences, churches, monasteries, and other public buildings on the slopes of a high hill, while the commercial quarter is spread out on the lower lands along the shore. The people in both these towns seem to have a great deal in common with the Greeks of classical times. Activity, energy, quick wit, and ability to take care of themselves form conspicuous traits of the population. Syra is said to be the most important town in the kingdom after Athens; and a walk among its streets and shops confirmed the impression formed in other towns where the Greeks evidently predominate, that no people are better able to manage their own business than these intellectual, practical, energetic, and open-minded descendants of the antique Achaians. They are surely among the most useful and efficient citizens of the modern world.

The next morning, as we were moving northward along the coast of Macedonia, the Thracian Olympus, with snowy summits, towered before our eyes in the west. It is a noble and most impressive group of mountains, and no one who sees it in a clear sunrise will condemn the early Greeks for making it the special abode of their divinities. Perhaps the Mysian Olympus, which rises above the Turkish city of Brusa, is grander, and certainly it is some thousands of feet higher; but it lacks the majesty and variety of its Thracian compeer.

We reached Salonica at about noon, and had ample time to drive to the city during the stay of the ship. Its appearance is very gay and cheerful, considering the amount of history that attaches to it. Here Xerxes had his camp on his way to overwhelm Greece; here Cassander, brother-in-law of Alexander the

Great, gave to the unconquered town the name of his wife, Thessalonica; here Cicero lived in exile; here was the Church of the Thessalonians to which St. Paul addressed two of the most interesting among his epistles. The place has now some one hundred and thirty thousand inhabitants. It has a considerable extension along the water front, and it reaches up the long slope of Mount Kortiash, quite far inland. I had always heard that it was rather dirty and disreputable, but we found it cheerful and reasonably clean in the beautiful sunshine of that lovely spring day. Among the people in the bustling streets the European element seemed to predominate, and I could not discover that the Turkish ownership gave to the city any special difference of physiognomy as compared with the more progressive towns of Greece.

Our next stopping place was to be Constantinople, and early in our stay at

Salonica the captain told me that two Turkish domestic establishments, one of them belonging to a Pasha, were coming on board as passengers for that metropolis. Presently the Pasha appeared, in a high hat and frock coat, altogether a European-looking gentleman; and with him arrived his ladies, one of them a handsome middle-aged woman, unveiled, looking like an Italian, with bright black eyes and pleasant bearing. She was followed by three others in semi-European costume, all wearing the *yashmak* or Turkish veil, which leaves the forehead and eyes uncovered, and hides the rest of the features. But what excited my interest particularly was the chief of the household, the principal eunuch, evidently an important personage, quite stout, and with a noble air of dignity, yet good-natured and friendly looking. For the two harems of our two distinguished passengers the captain opened separate gangways near the rudder-post aft, disclosing suites of cabins that we had not before suspected. As soon as the ship had started, the new inmates withdrew to their quarters and were seen no more until we were in Constantinople.

An interesting incident in our passage from Salonica was a pause for the Custom House visitation in the Dardanelles, which this time occupied perhaps two hours. It was varied by the arrival of the habitual boatload of fantastic pottery, which is made in that neighborhood, and is not only fantastic, but ugly. Yet everybody buys a specimen and carries it home as evidence of having been there. There is some display of military life at the Dardanelles, on both the Asiatic and European sides; but whether the showy forts are really formidable we could not tell and did not care much. It was far more engaging to the mind to gaze over the broad plain that lies toward the site of ancient Troy, and to imagine the ships and the fighters and the scenes there in the days of Achilles and Agamemnon.

We reached Constantinople the next morning, and, instead of being anchored out in the middle of the harbor, as had happened to us on former visits, we saw our ship tied to the wharf, and were able to walk ashore down an ordinary gangway. We had the day before us, and put it in first by a visit to the bazaar, which we found sadly modernized. The roof, which used to extend over the narrow and crooked passageways which ramify through it like streets, was gone, and an air of novelty and cleanness had succeeded the dirty and picturesque antiquity which we had seen there in former times. Our old friends, the dealers in carpets and bric-à-brac, were still there, however, and the coffee which they served was quite as enchanting as ever. Why is it that Turkish coffee is so much better than all others? It is a kind of potentialistic and transcendental preparation that other lands do not know and very poorly imitate.

From the bazaar we drove to St. Sophia, the most noble, most impressive, and most religious of religious structures—superior, I think, in its effect upon the soul to every other temple of worship. It is impossible to pass under its high arches or to cross its wide pavements without emotions of reverence and adoration. In one place, at a little distance from each other, were assembled two separate groups of students, all sitting upon the floor with the Koran in their hands, listening to the loud reading and exposition of their two professors, who would first give a passage from the sacred book, and then pause to explain and comment. The reading was apparently in Arabic, and I thought that the exposition was also in that language, but in this I may have been mistaken. The only point that I was quite sure of was that neither of the two schools seemed to be interfered with by the other, although the instruction in each was audible to the students of the other as well as to the strangers who stood around.

From St. Sophia we drove to the museum of antiquities at Seraglio Point. This is an institution which has existed more than forty years, but it is only in the last ten years that it has risen into serious importance. Now the law is that all objects of antiquity unearthed in any part of the Turkish empire must be brought here for preservation and exhibition, and an experienced antiquarian can spend a day profitably in examining the collection long since assembled.

But it was not until 1887 that the great discovery was made at Sidon which has raised the museum to high distinction among the famous collections of the great European cities. This discovery produced seventeen sarcophagi, the most important of them Greek, all of which are now to be seen here. One among them, known as the sarcophagus of Alexander the Great, excels all the others, and must be ranked among the most admirable remains of Grecian sculpture. Though there is no reason to believe that it was made for Alexander, it is called by his name because his effigy is conspicuous among its carvings. It is of white marble, perhaps a little less than six feet high, and all four of its sides are covered with the noblest style of Greek art. On one side a hunt is depicted, on the other side a battle, and each end has a battle scene. The entablatures, which are covered with these scenes, are perhaps two feet and a half in height. The figures are in high relief and in violent action, and, what is more remarkable, they are all gently tinted with delicate colors that add much to the effect, but do not injure the quality of the marble surface. It is one of the most wonderful works that have been recovered from antiquity, worthy of being matched with the Venus of Milo and the Hermes of Olympia. Precisely when it was made, or who was the artist who conceived and executed such a glorious production, is unknown. There is no mention or allusion in classical literature that indicates either its epoch or its authorship; but the traveller who has not seen it should pack his trunk as quickly as possible and take his tickets for the Golden Horn.

Our day was now well advanced, yet after St. Sophia and the museum and the bazaar it was still impossible to leave the place without driving around the ancient walls. Few things in all Europe are better worth seeing; and, if I were to visit the old city a thousand times, I should always wish to see them again. The day was lovely and our carriages were good, but the roughness of the streets was something that no one could imagine without driving through them. The further west you go and the nearer you approach to the ancient towers, the more precipitously rough, backward, forward, and sideways, the roads become. However, we lived through it, until we reached the head-waters of the Golden Horn. There, hiring a boat and rowers, we dismissed our shattering cabs and got back to our ship in time to make everything comfortable before she started to go up the Bosporus.

As we were passing out of the Golden Horn and turning our prow toward the north we came upon a lovely American yacht of perhaps three hundred tons, painted white and bearing the starry banner. What her name was and who was her owner we could not find out. But it was almost like seeing home once more, and all our hearts gave three cheers again and again.

The journey up the Bosporus from Constantinople to the Black Sea is among the spectacles that every traveller celebrates. We accomplished it in sunshine, and with the flowers of the peach trees and judas trees in full display. The distance is perhaps twenty-five or thirty miles, and the high and gently sloping and varied shores are covered with villas, palaces, gardens, and castles. It was indeed a delicious excursion. We entered the Black Sea before dark, and without further adventure found ourselves at Odessa the second morning afterward at about ten o'clock.

II.

THE RUSSIAN RIVIERA.

OUR ship had scarcely been fastened to the wharf at Odessa when a Russian officer came on board and informed me that orders had been given that our luggage was not to be subjected to Custom House examination, and, upon my inquiring the source of such politeness, I was told that it was done at the instance of Dr. Thomas E. Heenan, an old friend of ours, who for several years has been Consul of the United States at that port. Dr. Heenan appears to be *persona grata*, not merely with the Americans, English, French, and other foreigners at Odessa, but with the Russian officials and Russian society as well. He soon afterward came on board in person, and was most warmly welcomed. He informed us also of an amusing occurrence that had taken place an hour or two before, which we found afterward exploited at length and with a good deal of wit in the Odessa *Vaestnik*. The police had been informed that when our party arrived it would be their duty not only to receive us with marks of courtesy, but to escort us and our *impedimenta* to the hotel where lodgings had been secured for us. A Russian steamer had arrived pretty early in the morning, and the police officers inquired if there were any Americans among the passengers. Two gentlemen answering to the description were found, and, without further inquiry, they were informed that they were expected, that their trunks were to be passed unopened, and that the officers would at once conduct them to their lodgings. Surprised but not displeased by this intelligence, the two gentlemen, both of them merchants of some description hailing from Boston, immediately started for the hotel, but, on arriving there, they declared that the rooms to which they were shown could not be intended for two persons only, and so the mistake was found out. Thus the Odessa newspaper had a chance to laugh at the police, on account of this blunder, and the rare opportunity was well improved.

Odessa is indeed a very charming city, boasting some three hundred and fifty thousand inhabitants. Spread out over an elevated and rather irregular surface, it fronts the sea with a bluff perhaps seventy feet in height. Along the outer border of this bluff is a neat little park called a boulevard, much frequented by ladies and children. The streets are wide, the public buildings many of them very handsome, the private houses spacious and elegant. We spent a part of three or four afternoons at the athletic grounds furnished by the city, where cricket is played mainly by foreigners and lawn tennis cultivated by clubs of ladies and gentlemen. It was also our good fortune to attend a celebration in the cathedral on the day of the new emperor's coronation in Moscow. The singing was magnificent, as I have almost always found it in Russian Orthodox churches, though the choir consists of male voices alone and no instruments are allowed. A review in the adjoining public square after the Te Deum in the church was quite impressive, both for the martial appearance of the soldiers and the precision of their movements. Lieut.-Gen. Zelony, the political governor and military commander of the province, received us with extreme graciousness, recalling the time when, as a subordinate officer, he had visited New York with the Russian fleet toward the close of the civil war.

Leaving Odessa at about three in the afternoon by a Russian ship—and we are bound to say that these ships are elegant, comfortable, and satisfactory—we went directly to Sevastopol, landing in that famous seaport of the Crimea before noon the next day. The entrance into the inner harbor is broad and without any obstacle, and the city, which was destroyed in the Crimean War of 1854, now shows no scars of that calamity, but stretches out along its ridges and sunny slopes in a way most attractive and hospitable. Like the hotels of Russia in general, those of Sevastopol are spacious, clean, and in every way agreeable, and the drives around the town are picturesque and pleasing, quite apart from their interest as memorable scenes in modern history. In this latter respect, however, it is not too much to say that there is scarcely another place in Europe which can vie with this corner of the Crimea. The Malakoff, the Redan, the Mamelon, the vast field on the southeast that slopes toward Balaklava, the monuments that mark the charge of the Light Brigade, the cemeteries of the

English, the French, the Italians, and the Russian defenders of the place, perhaps the most gallant of all, and Balaklava itself, with its wonderful harbor, whose entrance is so narrow that two ships cannot navigate it together, absorb the mind with memories of that tremendous struggle, at once one of the most heroic and most useless wars of modern times; useless because it has left no permanent fruits, and the questions they fought about then are essentially the same as those which still confront the contending powers.

The immense historical interest of the Crimea has combined with a certain comparative inaccessibility to prevent the universal recognition of its extraordinary natural beauty and attractiveness as a semi-tropical region quite near to the Caucasus. But it was not until we had finished with the sights and the memories of Sevastopol and Balaklava that we came to appreciate the strange charm of the Crimea and the delight it has in store for travellers who are not too much in a hurry. Starting in the morning from Sevastopol and driving with one or two changes of horses, we traversed the southern projection of the peninsula, and at about two o'clock in the afternoon passed through the Gates of Baidar, as the passage through the Iaïla Mountains is called, and looked down upon one of the noblest spectacles in the world. Immediately before us lay the boundless sea, the shore rocky and broken, with villages, churches, castles, and little seaports, all made accessible by the great road cut into the mountain side here and there, and then built out upon walls over some abyss or valley below, alone enough to make the name of Prince Michael Worontzoff forever memorable in all southeastern Russia.

The vegetation on the mountain slopes toward the sea is wonderfully varied and interesting. The prevailing trees are oaks and beeches, with pinion pines, cypresses, myrtles, mulberry trees, and occasionally fig trees mingled among them. I was greatly impressed by a kind of dwarf beech which I had never seen in any other sylva, and of which we passed that day hundreds of specimens. It often lay stretched out almost flat upon the ground, and again where the soil and the exposure were favorable, it would assume a form of perfect regularity and rise to the height of six or eight feet. The leaves are exceedingly small and lustrous, making it a very decorative plant. It seems surprising that botanists have never brought it out to the knowledge of the world and made it available for general cultivation. Of the wild azaleas that we saw growing in the Crimea, and the Caucasus too, I am bound to add that they were rather poor and disappointing. Those of Pike County are ten times finer.

About five o'clock we reached Yalta,

an agreeable watering place with hotels, bath-houses, and other amusements, and perhaps fifteen hundred regular inhabitants. We stayed there three or four days, and one of our most interesting excursions was to Livadia, a country seat of vast extent belonging to the Czar. Getting permission from the commander of the guard, at the entrance, we spent a large part of a day in visiting it. There are several extensive dwellings, all simple and convenient, not furnished with any great magnificence, but sufficient for every requirement of comfort. In one bedroom of the imperial chateau we saw inserted in the parquetted floor a small cross of wood, marking the spot where the late Emperor Alexander III had died sitting in his chair.

We went through the greenhouses, finding them large, filled with many interesting yet not extraordinary plants, especially palms, but not otherwise remarkable. It was like the collection of a millionaire with no unusual taste and no extensive knowledge of botany or of the marvels of modern culture. The collection of orchids seemed peculiarly limited. The roads through the forest, which covers much of the estate, are perfectly good, but nothing more. There seemed, for instance, to be a scarcity of vistas taking advantage of the opportunity of looking out upon the adjoining sea. It was a case of magnitude, but not of high art.

There are several other famous estates in the vicinity, one or two of them belonging to members of the imperial family, but we did not attempt to visit them; and finally, having exhausted the interest of the shops in Yalta, and that is saying a good deal, we left the Crimea and its delightful climate one pleasant evening on a most excellent Russian ship, whose final destination was Batoum, the last Russian port at the eastern extremity of the Black Sea.

On the way we stopped first at

Kertch, the ancient Panticapœum at the entrance to the Straits of Yenikale and the Sea of Azov. It is a very pleasant place, with thirty odd thousand inhabitants and an important trade, especially in salt. The most interesting object here is the so-called tomb of Mithridates VII, or Mithridates the Great, next to Hannibal perhaps the most energetic and irreconcilable foe of ancient Rome. His tomb is a rather rococo structure on the summit of a hill which overlooks the city and the harbor. Excavations from the mounds about it, and elsewhere near the city, have contributed to the Imperial Museum in St. Petersburg and to the British Museum in London a quantity of gold ornaments which compel attention even among the manifold treasures of those rich and most instructive collections of antiquities. The share of the British Museum was sent there by Major Westmacott, of the British army, after the allies had captured Kertch in 1855, during the operations of the Crimean War.

We were able to drive nearly to the summit of the hill and to examine closely the ancient tomb. We found, however, that the territory surrounding it was still frequented by a number of amateur excavators, who, with long iron hooks, poke in the gravel to find antiquities that have escaped previous efforts. From one of these I bought for a few kopecks three or four little terra cotta images, which the seller assured me had been dug out on the spot; but, on careful examination, I found they had been made in Italy for sale as specimens of prehistoric art. We also visited the Museum in one of the streets near the water, but saw there nothing very impressive, the really valuable objects having long since been taken away. But the view from the summit of the hill was superb, and we greatly enjoyed our afternoon's stroll around the old tomb and down through the streets of the town. We saw plenty of shops for the sale of antiquities, all well provided with imitations of modern manufacture; but it was impossible to gaze from the summit of the hill over the vast country to the north and west without longing to break into some of the many large *kourgans*, or burial mounds of regular conical form, which dot the landscape in almost every direction.

I mentioned this to an expert upon our steamer, and he agreed with me as to the desire, but added that experience shows that where it is gratified the effort almost always results in disappointment. Most of these mounds, he said, are merely the graves of important individuals of prehistoric times. In the centre of the large ones is usually found a skeleton horse standing with a skeleton man on his back. This was a favorite mode of burial for the old Cimmerian chieftains, and very rarely, almost never, in fact, are ornaments of precious metals found among the relics; while the remains of pottery are usually of no value and of trifling interest.

We left the roadstead of Kertch before sundown, and the next morning found ourselves at Novorossisk, a noble harbor, with every point on the shores bearing evidence of the immense manufacturing and commercial activity which marks the business towns of modern Russia. A railway leads hence northwardly to Rostov-on-the-Don. New buildings seemed to be going forward everywhere, and the petroleum traffic, which has covered the whole southwestern shore of the Caucasian country with a series of the busiest places in the world, was evidently in full operation here. But our hope of seeing the great summits of the Caucasus was foiled. Both Elbruz and Kasbek were veiled by clouds, and so they remained during the whole day.

Our next stopping place was at Soukhoumkalé, and the next at Poti, at the mouth of the river Rion, likewise a place of extreme activity, with a branch of the Trans-Caucasian railway extending as far as Kutais, on the way to Tiflis and the Caspian. The Rion is the ancient Phasis, and hither the Argonauts came seeking the Golden Fleece, and hence they returned after they had got it. The low-lying, malarious-looking shores and the turbulent river, swollen to enormous extent by the spring freshets from the mountains, justified the description of the poet:

> He passed the sea,
> And reached a river opening into it,
> Across the which the white-winged fowl did flit
> From cliff to cliff, and on the sandy bar
> The fresh waves and the salt waves were at war
> At turning of the tide.
> . . . .
> Now swift beneath the oar strokes Argo flew,
> While the sun rose behind them, and they drew
> Unto the river's mouth, nor failed to see
> Absyrtus's galley waiting watchfully
> Betwixt them and the white-tipped turbid bar.
> Therefore they got them ready now for war
> With joyful hearts, for sharp they sniffed the sea

And saw the great waves tumbling green and free
Outside the bar upon the way to Greece,
The rough green way to glory and sweet peace.

 . . . .

But Jason, roaring as the lioness
When round her helpless whelps the hunters press,
Whirled round his head his mighty brass-bound spear
That, flying, smote the Prince beneath the ear,
As Arcas's arrow sunk into his side.
Then, falling, scarce he met the rushing tide
Ere Argo's mighty prow had thrust apart
The huddled oars, and through the fair ship's heart
Had thrust her iron beak, and the green wave
Rushed in, as rushed the waters through a cave
That tunnels half a sea-girt lonely rock.
Then, drawing swiftly backward from the shock,
And heeding not the cries of fear and woe,
They left the waters dealing with their foe;
And at the following ship threw back a shout
And seaward o'er the bar drave Argo out.

The gray sky and the heavy mists hiding the mountain-tops, and even obscuring the mighty forests of their slopes, were all sufficiently in harmony with these classical fancies of the ancient world; but the pervading odor of petroleum and the rush of business around the shore had nothing poetical or beautiful in their suggestions; and we were not sorry when our anchor was pulled up, and the Colchian hills behind us grew faint and fainter as our ship pushed southward toward Batoum.

III.

THE SOUTHERN ASPECTS OF THE CAUCASUS.

WE arrived at Batoum in good season the next morning, and our steamer passed within the great jetty which protects the harbor on the west. The anchorage is extensive and perfectly safe, with an adequate depth of water, but the place is said to be unwholesome, owing to the marshy nature of the country for a considerable distance inland. The town is fortified, and a considerable garrison seems to be kept there. We saw on all sides the same indications of active business, and smelled the same vivid odor of petroleum, which we had observed at the other ports looking eastward toward the great mountains and the Caspian. We soon had the pleasure of a visit from Mr.

James C. Chambers, Consul of the United States, to whom, as well as to Mr. Stevens, the British Vice-Consul, we were indebted for many acts of courtesy during our brief sojourn in the town.

Batoum is entirely a modern city in its appearance and arrangements, but all visitors are taken to visit the *zamok* or ruined chateau of Queen Thamara. Its remains occupy the summit of a moderate hill outside the town and about two miles from its centre. This Queen appears to have been a lady of considerable importance, and Mr. Freshfield speaks of her with some enthusiasm. " Queen Thamara," he says, " the Charlemagne of the Caucasian isthmus, at the close of the twelfth century spread Christianity among the Ossetes, and dotted their heights with churches." However that may have been, we found on the beautiful fresh turf which surrounds the fallen towers of her old castle, in the shade of the big trees, a most agreeable place for luncheon. But our desire to start for the interior prevailed over every other attraction. It was still early in the afternoon when we took our places in the train for Tiflis, the mountain railway over which we were to travel having at last been repaired, so that there was a prospect of getting through to the Georgian capital, though there had been no communication with it by train for a month or more.

We had scarcely got out of sight of Batoum when the clouds that had so long concealed the mountains disappeared, and we saw quite distinctly the long range extending apparently from west to east, Elbruz, with its double summits on the west, and in the east Kasbek, a marvel of beauty, worthy even to rival the solemn apparition of the Jungfrau, as one may behold it at sunrise from Interlaken. But Kasbek, if somewhat inferior in grandeur, is the more beautiful of the two, rising in a symmetrical though slender pyramid, as we now saw it at a distance of perhaps seventy-five miles; and though I do not like to compare the Caucasus with the Alps, my sober judgment is that, of all the great mountain displays, there cannot be any more noble, more beautiful, or more impressive than these wonders of eastern Europe. But on this subject let us pause for a moment, and listen to the great poet of Russia:

THE CAUCASUS.

Caucasus below me! Alone on the height
I stand above the snows, on the brink of these awful
  steeps.
An eagle rising from a distant summit
Floats immovably on a level with me.
Here I behold the birth of rivers
And the first moving of the terrible avalanches.
Here the clouds hover quietly beneath me;
Through them I hear the roaring waterfalls;
And see the naked hugeness of the rocks;
Lower down, the thin mosses, the dry shrubs;
And there also the green shades of the forests,
Where the birds chatter, where the deer leap.
There also men build nests in the mountains
And the sheep crawl over the grassy declivities,

And the shepherd climbs down into the pleasant valleys
Where the Aragva rushes against the shaded shore,
And the poor horseman hides himself in some crevice.
There the beautiful Terek with fury
Plays and roars, like a young wild beast
Struggling with hunger to escape his iron cage;
And he rushes against the banks, with useless raging,
And licks the rocks with hungry wave.
In vain! There is no food for him, no consolation,
And the dumb crags compress him terribly.

THE MONASTERY ON KASBEK.

High over the family of mountains,
Kasbek, thy imperial tent
Gleams with eternal splendors.
Thy monastery behind the clouds,
Like a shrine descending from heaven,
Floats, scarcely visible, above the summits.
Oh, distant, longed-for shore,
There, bidding farewell to all below,
Let me rise to supreme freedom!
There in a cell, cloud-enveloped
Hide me in the neighborhood of God!

On our way to Tiflis we passed without much delay over the place where the railway had just been restored, and arrived at our destination before nine o'clock in the evening. Yet the next day the rails were broken again, and during the week that we remained in Tiflis there was not a day when a train could be sent to Baku on the Caspian; and thus we were constrained to give up the idea of making a visit to Central Asia and to the old city of Tamerlane.

In the strict sense, the Caucasus is a body of mountains parallel to the coast of the Black Sea, beginning on the west at Anapa, near the Sea of Azov, and extending in a southeasterly direction to Cape Abcheran on the Caspian. The length of the mass is about seven hundred miles, and its breadth varies from seventy miles to one hundred and fifty. Mount Elbruz, the highest elevation in Europe, is pretty nearly in the centre of the chain, and Kasbek, the next in height, is about sixty miles to the east of Elbruz; and there are a great number of other peaks of almost equal importance.

The Russian political divisions, which

are attached to the Caucasus and are generally known as Cis-Caucasia and Trans-Caucasia, make together about two hundred thousand square miles of territory, with an aggregate population at present of perhaps eight million souls of various races and numerous religions. Among the aboriginal inhabitants of this country there are said to be some sixty or seventy different tribes, speaking as many different tongues and dialects, living mainly by agriculture and the chase, and carrying on various domestic manufactures, generally marked with the stamp of high artistic instinct—such as the weaving of rugs and carpets, the making of a peculiar kind of silverware ornamented with black inlaying, known as *niello*, and the making of swords and daggers, as well as of woollen cloth, felt, and articles of Astrakhan fur. In fact, foreign manufactures, except those of Central Asia, seem as yet to have gained very little foothold in this region.

A good illustration of the artistic genius of the people is a piece of the native pottery, which I bought at an insignificant railway station in the hills between Kutais and Tiflis, and which evinces the art impulse in a remarkable degree. There is nothing like it in any European collection. I had never seen a specimen before except at the Czar's country seat of Livadia, where there is one standing on a mantelpiece. The pottery is coarse enough, but the glaze is of a beautiful peachblow color, and the design and decorations are really original and striking.

The people themselves, as they are seen in the cities and villages, are apparently, for the most part, what is called half-civilized. They are very handsome, athletic, and graceful. The women have always been famous for their beauty. As for the Caucasian gentleman, he has all the distinction and dignity of appearance and manners that belong to the character of a gentleman in the most civilized countries.

In all this region there is only one road leading through the mountains from south to north—namely, the Georgian military road, so called. It starts in the south from Tiflis, passes the foot of Kasbek, and continues through the Darial Pass to Vladikavkaz, a distance of two hundred and one versts, or about one hundred and thirty miles. The railway from Novorossisk to Rostov-on-the Don turns the western extremity of the mountains, but does not cross them; and the railway, five hundred and sixty miles in length, from Batoum and Poti through Tiflis to Baku on the Caspian, turns the southeastern extremity of the range in the same manner. This railway, by the way, running along mountain gorges, with no well-defined natural line to follow, is in many places built on masonry supports, and at almost every turn is subject to serious damage from freshets.

But the Georgian military road, following almost a direct line, crosses the mountains through what seems to be the one available north and south pass; it is macadamized, about one hundred feet in width, and is kept in perfect condition.

The capital of this vast and little known region is Tiflis, with perhaps three hundred and fifty thousand people, and still growing, as new buildings going up here and there afford very sure evidence. This picturesque town was the capital of Georgia in old times, and here the Russian Governor-General, the military authorities, and the judicial tribunals have their seat. As befits an Alpine metropolis, it is planted in the valley of the Kour, a rushing mountain torrent which falls sixty feet or more in its passage through the town, and occasionally wears away a bit of the shore and tumbles down a house or two. The day we got there the river had furiously attacked a small island opposite our hotel. The public excitement was intense. Crowds gathered on the bridge just below the island, and a gang of laborers was hard at work getting out a quantity of goods that were stored in a wooden building on the island. The goods were carried away, and the building was almost taken to pieces ready for removal, when the water fell, and the danger was over for the time.

IV.

TIFLIS AND TRANS-CAUCASIA.

THERE are no big mountains close at hand at Tiflis, but in every direction the place is surrounded by heights whose rocks sometimes stand out naked and pictorial without any earthy covering, while one or two have monasteries on their summits, which must be very difficult for the monks to climb. On one of the more gentle among these heights there is the ancient wall of a citadel inclosing perhaps a dozen acres, whose well-grassed interior now performs the useful function of pasturing a few sheep, and serving as a lounging place for any unoccupied travellers who may like to wander over it in a pleasant afternoon. Just below this on the east is a large slope containing what is called a botanic garden, though it is difficult to find among its alleyways any great variety of plants or any sharp scientific arrangement. In this vicinity also, on the steep declivities of several hills, are what I took to be the cabins of the early inhabitants—curious bird-cages of abodes, clinging one above another to the sides and irregularities of the rocks, and reached from below by queer and erratic stairways. In the levelled valley-bottoms among these ancient eyries modern streets and rows of buildings have everywhere made their way, so that there is now very little space in what we will call the native quarter remaining to be occupied.

On the same side of the river—and I am speaking of the right-hand bank as you go with the stream—are the most important public buildings, all modern and substantial, the palaces of the Governor-General and of the military commander, the museum, and a whole array of public offices, as well as the Court House, which last I had the good fortune to visit in company with his Excellency the Chief Judge. We happened upon a very interesting scene in the Court House, and a very unusual one, even in Russia. The proclamation of the new Czar announcing his accession to the throne contained, as usual, a clause providing for a certain reduction in the sentences of all criminals already condemned by the courts; and we entered the court room at Tiflis just as the members of the court, with the exception of the President, were taking their seats to apply this act of grace in the cases of perhaps twenty men who had been tried recently and had not yet taken their departure for their places of punishment. I did not count the number of the judges upon the bench, but I should say that there were four or five of them, all dressed in a kind of semi-military uniform such as I had never seen worn by judges elsewhere. The criminals were made to stand up in line on the left hand of the court. The clerk called their names, and each individual was identified. Then the imperial decree was read, and the amount of reduction in punishment was written down for each, after which they were removed from the court room under guard. They were not an attractive set of characters, though they were mostly young men, and the proceedings did not seem to have much interest for them. I asked the Chief Judge what was the nature of their offences, and he said that they were brigands or highwaymen. The proceeding was grave enough, but it lacked the formality and the solemnity which it might have worn in the court rooms of some other countries.

The museum is a very attractive establishment, with collections of animals, birds, plants, minerals, primitive human habitations, and everything available to illustrate the natural history of the Caucasus, and the modes of life prevailing among the earlier inhabitants of the country, as well as those of the present day. It is under the learned direction of Dr. De Raddé, and its arrangement and classification are practical and instructive. The establishment fills the three floors of a large building, and also extends into an adjoining garden, where it occupies a great deal of space.

In Tiflis, as in every other Oriental or semi-Oriental town, the most interesting lounging place is the bazaar. As a mart for Oriental carpets, embroideries, silks, gauzes, and so on, Tiflis is as good as any other place, and perhaps better than most—better, I might almost say, than Constantinople itself. All sorts of Eastern rugs—cheap, dear, commonplace, and of high art—are to be found there in abundance. But, strange to say, it takes perseverance and determination to get at them. I never saw traders who seem so indifferent to the chances of selling; and I would advise my friends who may go there to get some important banker, or wholesale dealer or other commercial magnate, to go with them to the bazaar and overawe the dealers so that they will bring out their best wares. This is especially the case with carpets and embroideries. If you are looking for silver goods, or weapons, or Caucasian hats, you may find merchants who will exhibit their whole stock and allow you to choose what you want without attempting to make you buy the less salable articles; but among the undisguised old Orientals, Hindoos, for example, it is not easy to get a sight of the best in the shop, and not so easy to buy it after it has been shown. They will ask you twice the genuine price and stick to it as if their salvation depended on it; and when they come down to bedrock, they show that they are doing you a favor which only a life of peace and humility ever afterward on your part can justify. However, the dealers in Oriental merchandise are numerous and their stores very extensive, and you can loiter and chatter and bargain in them day after day with perpetual amusement and the agreeable conviction that you are not so much cheated after all. One delightful old Persian *hadji*, who thought he spoke French, and from whom after several visits I bought some little traps, embraced me as we parted, exclaiming effusively: "Oh, mon cher amant!" and I am sorry I may never see him again.

What Tiflis seems to lack is means of amusement. If there is a theatre there, I did not find it out, and the only substitute seemed to be the occasional divertisements of two or three concert gardens. We went to one of these one evening. The garden was very large and partially lighted, consisting mainly of alleyways opened among clumps of trees and shrubbery; and the public was not numerous. We heard with attention a concert of Armenian instrumental music, but its prevailing sentiment was rather sad and its technical perfections were limited.

The time to move on having come, we went to the office of the postal establishment to make arrangements for the journey northward. Not merely the transportation of the mails, but also the carrying of passengers over the Georgian military road, is in the hands of the Government, and we went to the office duly fortified with certifications of introduction. It was situated beside an immense yard with an extraordinary array of carriages of different kinds. Stating to the official in charge the number of our party and the time when we desired to start, he advised us to examine the carriages and select those we might prefer. Accordingly we chose for our principal vehicle what they call a *kareta*. It is a big and heavy conveyance swung upon leather straps such as we used to call Concord thorough-braces, and requiring six horses to draw it. In front is the driver's seat, wide enough to hold two or three persons. Behind and above, under a projecting hood, there is a seat with room for three passengers. Back of this, and still higher on the top, is the place for luggage, and the size of this can be estimated when I say that the baggage of our whole party, seven to ten heavy trunks, was firmly packed there and fastened so that it could not move. Underneath, in the centre of the vehicle, is a coupé, with glass windows on each side, in which three persons can be transported; and behind the body of the coach is a seat for a single individual, apparently intended for a guard. With the passengers, the luggage, the driver, and the guide, whose duty is to supervise the expedition and to see to getting fresh horses whenever they may be necessary, the whole outfit—horses, carriage, and contents—must have weighed about eight tons, and it turned out that a very comfortable mode of travelling it was.

In addition to the *kareta*, with its six horses, and I should mention that four of these were on the wheel and two in the lead, we took a two-horse carriage like an English phaeton, in which three or four passengers could conveniently find room. Our party had become considerably enlarged beyond its first dimensions by the presence of one or two English gentlemen and also by that of a new Italian Minister to Persia, who was obliged, owing to the impossibility of getting to Baku by rail, to go through the mountains and to Astrakhan, in order to find a steamboat which would take him across the Caspian.

Before leaving New York, my friend, Mrs. MacGahan, had advised me to secure, if possible, the services of Alexander Mamatsett as our guide from Tiflis to Vladikavkaz, and we were fortunate enough to find him disengaged. He is a giant, dark, evidently a Georgian, dressed in Caucasian costume, and speaking only his native language and Russian; and when my statement that I had asked for him on the advice of Mrs. MacGahan was translated to him, a smile spread over his features as he said, "Oh, yes; I remember her with pleasure, and shall be delighted to be of service to any friend of hers."

The next morning at nine o'clock we started with a bright sunshine, though the mountains in the distance were still covered with clouds which made them invisible. Our six horses seemed at first rather light for so heavy a cargo, but the pace at which we set out was lively. We had scarcely got out of the city when we overtook two or three trains of carts, and when they did not get out of the way rapidly enough Mamatsett would take the big whip from the hand of our coachman and lay it over the shoulders of the delaying cartmen. The first one he struck turned in a rage, but the moment he saw who it was his anger seemed to disappear, and he took his flogging with meekness and almost with an expression of satisfaction.

About fifteen miles from Tiflis we came upon the old town of Mtskhet, formerly one of the capitals of Georgia, a place of very curious interest, bearing all the marks of extreme antiquity. The cathedral is described as built in the fourth century, and a number of the Bagratide kings are said to be buried there. Tamerlane destroyed it at the end of the fifteenth century, but it was rebuilt a hundred years or so later. A striking feature of Mtskhet, as of other important Georgian towns, is a great number of ancient towers rising to a height of sixty or eighty feet, belonging apparently to different antique strongholds, and scattered all about the heights and hillsides as if to look out for some approaching foe. As we did not belong to that category, we drove off with some regret at our inability to stay long enough to explore, at least, the cathedral and the royal tombs.

During the rest of the day we passed many cultivated farms, all on elevations considerably above the road, where the farmers were busy ploughing small fields, or making their earliest crop of hay; and they were good farmers, too, judging by the neatness with which their work was done. As the afternoon wore on, we came into a land where the grass in the valleys was very lovely; where the forests were made up of large trees richly furnished with foliage; and we began to get misty glimpses of the great central chain of the Caucasus.

Thus the scenery was extremely varied, picturesque and beautiful. The Aragva presently became its most attractive feature, now flowing smoothly through meadows, and now roaring in ravines and cataracts. Our chief attention, however, was given to that famous piece of engineering, the military road, also a monument of the genius of Prince Michael Woronzoff. For a mountain highway nothing better could be imagined. Winding along the edge of the river or climbing over a hill where the solid rock had been blasted or carved out to make room for the roadway, it was everywhere of equal width, thoroughly macadamized, smooth and even, and kept in perfect repair in every part. We saw workmen at a dozen places during that day's drive putting in new masses of broken stone to fill up inequalities, and rolling them down with heavy machines.

As soon as we got fairly away from the city's traffic, we began to drive like fury. Up hill or down, the rate of going was almost always the same, and sometimes when going down it became rather alarming to the nerves. As the road had to follow the inequalities of the mountains, and in many places was carried out around projecting crags, it was impossible to see whether or not other carriages were coming to meet us on the other side of the projection. On the one hand was the solid wall of the mountain, and on the other a precipice of perhaps five hundred or a thousand feet down. On the outer side of the road, the side toward the precipice, there was everywhere a solid stone wall laid in mortar and about three feet high; but if, when rushing down hill at the rate of twelve miles an hour, your equipage, weighing so many tons, should strike in turning a corner upon another carriage and cargo, whether heavier or lighter, the result would be a collision, and the wall of three feet in height would not avail to prevent one party or the other from bouncing over the precipice. This consideration did not seem to occur either to Mamatsett or the coachman, and as we approached some of these little turns it was impossible not to imagine that this time we might catch up with disaster;

yet there was never any real trouble. Our fears always proved to be groundless, and we swung around the projection of the mountain just as smoothly on the lower side as we had swung toward it on the upper. Yet it made an exciting and breakneck sort of coaching, and we were very glad when at night, after having completed half the length of the military road, we stopped before the comfortable post-house in the old Georgian village of Mleta.

When we delivered the official recommendation which we had procured at Tiflis, advising the keeper of the post-house that the reserved imperial apartments were to be opened for our use, he said: "I am very sorry, but, unfortunately, you come a little too late. His Excellency the Persian Minister, with his suite, arrived here an hour ago on his way home from the coronation at Moscow; and we have been obliged to put him in possession of those apartments;

however, we think that we can make you comfortable, and that you will not have to undergo any serious inconvenience."

So it turned out for the whole party, excepting the Italian Minister to Persia, whose lodgings were inferior to the average. But when I condoled with him the next morning, he said that he had slept perfectly, and that there was really nothing to lament in the incident.

V.

THROUGH THE DARIAL PASS TO ROSTOV.

As we drove out of the post-house yard at Mleta the next morning, disturbing one or two lazy and dishevelled camels that were loafing about the stable doors, we perceived that at last we had before us some real mountain climbing. Crossing the south-flowing Aragva on a stone bridge, we began the long ascent of the hill which stands opposite to Mleta. The road was precisely of the same breadth and style as we had travelled upon the day before, but it wound backward and forward up the hillside in long reaches, with a continuous rise that put rapid driving out of the question. The spectacle, however, was altogether superb, and we were glad to study it slowly.

Below us lay the village we had just left. Behind it rose another mountain of more moderate dimensions than that we were ascending. In its cultivated spots and its many little hay fields the farmers were making the most of the morning. Further along to the northeast an old castle stood out upon crags that projected above the river; and the imagination could easily go back to the time when these pristine strongholds had each its garrison of freebooters, and fighting, plundering and devastation were the rule and the business of the land. But now all was peace and repose. There was no garrison, no military display, and no flag flying from any pinnacle. There was no indication that even a policeman was within call, yet every one felt that the power which had reduced the half-savage tribes of the mountains to order, was there to maintain and protect the civilization whose foundations it had laid.

It was a long as well as a slow road,

and presently, as we approached the summit, the snows began to appear in heavy drifts along the sides of it. When we reached our first change of horses we had nearly gained the ridge of the Krestovaya Gora, the "mountain of the crosses," so called because two stone crosses have been erected there, one of them very ancient, attributed to Queen Thamara, and the other a modern creation of sixty years ago. There is a village of some shops and several houses, with an attractive old church that invites the traveller to come in and say his prayers. The height of this mountain, by the way, is eight thousand feet above the sea level, and it is only a short distance beyond the summit that the descent begins, leading down into the valley of the impetuous north-flowing Terek, and through a series of mountain landscapes of peerless and almost inexpressible magnificence.

From the top of the Krestovaya Gora,

past Kasbek, through the gorge of Darial, until the crossing of the mountains is completed and we find the Terek flowing in peace and quiet through green meadows near Vladikavkaz, the very opposite of the fury with which it forces itself among the mountain reefs, there is a continuous scene of rocky peaks, of noble mountain openings and gorges, of portentous overshadowing cliffs, of broken and dilapidated old castles, which make of this roadway of forty or fifty miles one of the wonders and marvels of the earth. It is impossible to think of it without longing to be there again, dashing along the riverside and through the narrow mountain defiles, with the same spirited horses, and the same enthusiastic giant of a Caucasian guide. The traveller who has not yet had this experience, is to be envied provided it is still in his power to procure it for himself; and he or she to whom it is possible and who does not at once set out to drive over the Krestovaya Gora, and through the Darial Pass, is to be pitied indeed.

We arrived in the village of Kasbek at about one o'clock, but the glory of the mountain was all hidden in the clouds. Even the monastery, which is at a point on the mountain's flank about eighteen hundred feet higher than the village, could not be seen; and it was not possible even to speculate at what elevation the ancient story had fixed the point where Prometheus was chained to the rock and vultures came to torment him. These were serious privations for which a very good luncheon afforded no satisfactory indemnity. But all such losses seemed trivial when we resumed our drive and began once more to pass between the barriers of the ever-varying peaks which hemmed in our way on either side.

These peaks rose on the east and west to a height of four thousand to six thousand feet above the level of the road.

They were bare, sharp-pointed, and often as slender in appearance as a man's fingers held up against the light; and far below them the massive forest came down almost to the river along whose banks we were driving. It was a tremendous, an amazing, spectacle, and we were through with it altogether too soon.

About three o'clock we came to an enlargement of the narrow valley, with a little low fort of queer construction, evidently designed to block the road against an enemy. A little further on, at the other end of the same enlargement, there was another fort of similar construction. Some one said that these forts were built by Schamyl in his struggle to maintain the independence of his Mohammedan tribe, and to continue his war against the power of Russia. We gazed at the fortifications with renewed interest; but I believed the story was altogether a fiction, and on looking in the books I am confirmed in this conclusion. Very likely Schamyl may have made a stand in the Darial Pass, at some period, but he could not have remained there for any length of time. That vital artery has long been too important for Russia to allow such an enemy to hold it even for a day; and, besides, the last desperate effort of Schamyl was made much further east, at Ghunib, in Daghestan, where Prince Bariatinski took him prisoner, and put an end to his wild dream of an independent Mohammedan State in the Caucasus.

If the passage of the mountains was like a battle in the intensity of its interest and its excitement, the arrival at Vladikavkaz was like the repose which follows after a victory won. With its forty-odd thousand people, Vladikavkaz is not exactly a Russian or a Caucasian town, but has qualities of both, and is rather like a holiday that comes between days of toil and agitation. The site is level; not even hills are visible, except at a distance, and the two or three long and quiet streets, stretching at right angles to each other, suggest repose and rest. Yet I am bound to say that the shops are peculiarly attractive from the number of Oriental and Caucasian articles that are offered in them. There is no such extreme variety as at Tiflis, but with patience and perseverance you may pick up little things that you have not been able to procure in the metropolis; and, finally, when you take your seat in the train for Rostov-on-the-Don you are freshened with the consciousness of an enterprise rounded out successfully, and completed to your satisfaction.

One of the best views of the great Caucasian chain is that gained from the railway to Rostov; and while the snowy summits of Elbruz form its most conspicuous feature, the long line of lofty and broken peaks and of massive forest-covered slopes remains in the memory as one of the grandest objects in nature.

Equal, however, in interest is the succession of Cossack villages planted along the line of the railway, and doubtless throughout the province, at pretty regular intervals. According to the latest official figures, there are about eight hundred thousand of these people along the Don, and very interesting people I found them to be. Known to the outside world chiefly as cavalry soldiers, those who have had an opportunity of seeing them at home, or have read what has been written about them, and, above all, that wonderful Cossack novel of Gogol's, "Taras Boulba," or Tolstoï's "Cossacks," understand that they are not without some of the most lasting and admirable traits of human nature. As we saw them in the country of the Don, agriculture is their main occupation, and no one would imagine that they were warriors also. The country is what an Illinois man would describe as rolling, with ridges of no great elevation here and there, but mainly level. The soil seemed black and rich, but when we passed over it the spring crops had scarcely been planted. The herds of cattle were large, and each herd had two or three men and dogs to keep it from wandering too far. There appeared to be no fences to mark the boundaries of the estates. The houses were small, and every village had its church. The general aspect of the land and people was peaceful, and it looked as if any form of political or intellectual agitation was out of the question there.

We were now beginning the railway part of our excursion, and this is the place to speak of the Russian railways. I have travelled upon them at various seasons and in various directions, and I testify that they are safe, comfortable, and agreeable. In this journey from Vladikavkaz to Rostov the distance is about four hundred and thirty miles, and it is made by the postal trains in about twenty-four hours, or, including stops, at the rate of twenty miles an hour. The tracks are always solid and smooth, and the cars are excellent. They are much wider than ours—wide enough, in fact, to admit of an inclosed corridor running the whole length of the car on one side, with doors opening into all the compartments. These are spacious enough, with two rows of broad seats facing each other and extending across the compartment at right angles to the corridor, though, except at night, only the bottom seats are used. These seats are long enough and wide enough for a large person to lie in comfortably when the beds are made up. The traveller takes as many places as he desires, and, if he wishes for the exclusive use of a compartment, he pays for it and has it. Russian people when travelling take with them their own sheets and rugs; but sheets and pillows can always be procured in a perfect state of cleanliness and at a reasonable charge from the porter in the car. The sleeping seems to be better than in our most luxurious sleeping cars. The lavatory arrangements are also satisfactory, and the neatness of the whole establishment leaves nothing to be desired. In fact, I have never seen any reason to complain of this part of the Russian railway arrangements. The journey to Rostov, and the subsequent longer journey from there to Moscow, landed us at our destinations with less fatigue and less disturbance of the nerves than we should be likely to experience in going from New York to Chicago or to Omaha.

I don't think that dining cars are known upon the Russian railways; at any rate I have never seen them; but the restaurants in the station houses are pleasant, and the stops are long enough to allow you to get what you want. You can take a seat at the table or refresh yourself standing; and at almost every station you can procure those incomparable products of the Russian cuisine, *stchy* and *borsh*. There is nothing in the culinary science of any other land known to me to be compared with these two kinds of soup. The *stchy* has for its essential element cabbage, and the *borsh* is based upon beets. What other materials go in with these I shall not undertake to say, except that beef plays a great rôle in the drama of the *stchy;* and, as *borsh* is white when it is served, I suspect that there may be milk in it. Yet I solemnly declare that, having procured an authoritative Russian cook book, and having myself carefully studied the prescriptions for both these works of art, and accurately translated the same, I have not yet succeeded in finding any Western *cuisinier* or *cuisinière* who could make and serve them in a style that would please an international expert. But while I am saying this, it is my duty to add that there is also another Russian soup which I have heard much celebrated in that empire, namely, the *botvinia*. It is white and is served cold, and I detest it.

But without pausing to debate these recondite subjects, let us not forget one article that is always to be found at every railway restaurant in Russia, as in every palace and every hut, always in transcendent perfection, such as all other peoples are not able to rival. I mean tea. An express train sends its hundred passengers into a commonplace railway station, and standing on a vast counter before them are a hundred glasses of tea. Some have thin slices of lemon for those who like that condiment; and others are served simply with as much sugar as you like; or, if you want a drop of cream, you can get that too; but the tea itself is something ecstatic, and you may voyage all around the earth from London to Formosa, and then back to

Dover, and never find any tea of such beautiful, inexplicable, delightful, living exquisiteness. What is the secret? Why is it that other lands and peoples continue to exist in such comparative disability? I cannot guess; but I know that a glass of Russian tea, or a cup of it, if you like that better, is something to enchant an ascetic and to rejuvenate an antediluvian.

Rostov stands on high land at the head of the Sea of Azov, a curious body of water, too shallow to be much navigated by large ships, yet of great importance from its fisheries and its trade in grain, wool, and cattle. We saw it in the fullness of the spring freshet, when the Don had flooded an immense extent of land between the railway embankment and the sea. A great mass of shipping was lying at the wharves, and it was evident that the place was full of business. Taganrog, which is about twenty miles further west, used to be more important, but Rostov now seems to be monopolizing the commerce of the region. One would not describe Rostov as a very charming or attractive town, but when we came to drive through its streets and to see what was there, we found it far from commonplace or uninteresting. Its population is now about one hundred thousand, mainly Russians, of course, but including a large representation of the business men of other nations. We remained there three days, and went away with the wish that we could have explored it more completely.

VI.

NIJNI, THE NEW CITY.

FROM Rostov to Nijni-Novgorod takes a pretty long time, with the slow railways of Russia. The distance is over a thousand miles, and naturally everybody breaks the journey by stopping in Moscow. Moscow is certainly one of the most engaging towns in the world, and no intelligent foreigner can go there as often as he would wish, or stay there as long. But our first purpose was with Nijni-Novgorod, because the annual semi-oriental fair was about to begin there. Besides, a vast exhibition of Russian industry and art had been organized under the patronage of the Government and was already in full operation. Accordingly, without any unnecessary delay, we found ourselves at Nijni, quartered in one of the extensive hotels upon the high land which, for living purposes, forms the official and more desirable, as well as the more picturesque, part of the city.

In its physical outlines Nijni-Novgorod is not dissimilar to Kiev. There is a long and broad elevation on the right bank of the two rivers, curving toward the south. At the foot of this elevation and following its curvature is the great river, the united Oka and Volga at Nijni, and the Dnieper at Kiev. Beyond the river, on its left bank, extends an immense plain, the deeper and lower part of the prehistoric sea which, as geologists assure us, once spread over the greater portion of Russia; and on this plain immense forests stretch away and finally lose themselves on the northern and eastern horizon. The Volga, however, is a much larger stream than the Dnieper, and in its volume and its swiftness it reminds the spectator of the Mississippi or the Missouri, except that its waters are clearer. Indeed, when we were at Nijni there seemed to be no mud at all mixed with them. On both of these rivers steamboats are numerous, but the navigation of the Volga is much the more important of the two. At Nijni you will find boats nearly equal to the largest on Long Island Sound, or to those giants that thirty years ago abounded on the Mississippi; and if you wish to go to Astrakhan and to take passage down the Caspian, one of these boats is to be preferred to the railway. They are spacious, clean, comfortable, and the passenger is well fed and transported much more speedily than when he undertakes to ascend the stream by the same conveyance.

The famous annual fair was only commencing when we got there; and although we spent a great deal of time wandering about in the passages and corridors of its buildings, it certainly did not come up, as an Oriental show, to the descriptions which we had been in the habit of reading. However, in the few days we remained it improved continually by arrivals from Central Asia and Persia, and we went away convinced that it would still prove worthy of its ancient renown.

But the exposition of Russian industries, on the other hand, far surpassed any idea we had formed about it. A vast array of adequate and suitable buildings had been erected for it, all on low lands on the left bank of the river, and it seemed to have attained, as if by magic, an astonishing magnitude and variety of development. The exhibition of silks, for instance, was amazing, and by silks I mean dress goods for ladies, brocades for house furnishing—in fact, every kind of silken fabric that modern luxury requires and modern art produces. If the looms and the skill of France were exerted to the utmost, I am sure they could not furnish a richer or more varied show than was displayed here at Nijni. It was really surprising, not merely for the multiplicity and fertility of the artistic genius it displayed, but also for the quantities of goods exhibited; and the same astonishment was produced by the examination of many other parts of the show. Woollen cloths of every description and of the most elegant finish were there in abundance and variety, and all from Russian looms; so also were ordinary carpetings. Articles of metal, arms, cutlery, samovars, the whole round of goods manufactured from platinum, iron, steel, and brass at Tula, were here in full force. So were laces, ribbons, shoes, millinery, jewelry, enamelled gold and silver; in short, whatever goes to the decoration of modern society seems to be produced in Russia in just as many styles and just as admirable as in any of the older and more practised countries; and when you turn to the ruder arts—such as the making of cordage, or the tanning of leather, or the weaving of sail cloth—it was all the same. Perhaps Russia cannot produce all these things quite as cheaply as France or Germany or England, but she produces them of just as high quality, with taste as refined and subtle, and in quantities sufficient to supply all her own needs, if not the needs of all her neighbors. In respect of what may be called art manufactures especially it was an amazing, almost a bewildering exhibition, and we felt that Germany, France, Austria, Italy, and England will presently have to face a new and formidable competitor in the world's manufacturing contest.

Two or three special buildings were devoted to the productions of Siberia. A great deal of space was given to an exhibition of the minerals peculiar to that country, and the collection was marked as belonging to the Czar. Of articles made by the natives—such as weapons, fishing apparatus, snowshoes, houses, rude household furniture, and so forth—there was an ample and most interesting display.

One of the most important departments was occupied by an immense assemblage of oil paintings by Russian artists. I do not remember precisely how many canvases there were, but I should say not less than five hundred. Very few of them were by our old acquaintances the Verestschagins, the Makaroffs and the other artists who have gained places for themselves in the galleries of the world. Not having made any notes on the spot, I cannot now remember the names of the individual painters, or attempt to describe their pictures; but many of them were such as would be admitted in any international exhibition. The simple truth is that the Russian school of painting is just as well established, and just as original and individual, as the German or the French; and it must be considered henceforth in any survey of the progress and achievements of the art.

The department of machinery did not seem to be so complete or so various as I should have expected to find it in any other of the great countries. But it was most interesting; and, regarded as an industrial product only partially developed, it seemed most encouraging, though I am not an expert and cannot undertake to pronounce a decided judgment. Another building, whose contents I studied with great attention, was that devoted to Chinese productions. This was the only building, it seemed, in which Russia could not claim to have produced at least the main part; and I am bound also to add that it was rather disappointing. A considerable space was occupied by porcelain and pottery, modern, of course, and it was not very remarkable, to say the least. Various kinds of grain were exhibited, including rice and wheat. But, perhaps, the most satisfactory display was that of silk goods, and especially of fabrics of raw silk. Even with the most critical examination it was impossible to discover that China has yet entered in any marked degree into the modern industrial competition of the Western nations.

Very extensive arrangements for the accommodation of visitors had been made in the neighborhood of the exhibition. Immense caravansaries of lodging houses had been erected, and they were of wood. In fact, the whole space at the command of the authorities was packed closely with these inflammable structures, and the idea of a fire among them was most disturbing. So we left Nijni on our way back to Moscow rather sooner than we had intended, and yet those buildings are still there, and no conflagration among them has been reported.

VII.

MOSCOW AND WARSAW.

Is it possible in any form of language to describe Moscow? Is there any artist of the pen who can reproduce in his page the marvels of form and color which express so much of the fascination that belongs to this historic city? It is a miracle, this interfusion of ancient and modern, this kaleidoscope of Asia and Europe contending but neither conquered, this unfinished history of a thousand years; and it cannot be fully portrayed by any efforts of mere phraseology or analysis. Besides there are more places in and about Moscow that a stranger ought to visit than any other capital can boast of; and a month might well be occupied in seeing them. Yet, let me try to point out some of the more salient and impressive features of the scene, and with them, perhaps, some of the more remarkable characteristics of the Russian people; and in doing this I shall endeavor to speak only of facts, and not of the inferences or suggestions of others.

The heart of Moscow is the Kremlin, and whatever injuries it may have received when Napoleon attempted to destroy it, they have all been obliterated by most careful restoration. The Kremlin is the ancient citadel, a fortress surrounded by a wall of undetermined antiquity a mile and a quarter in length, high and solid enough to resist cavalry and infantry, but not artillery. Within this wall are several churches, two imperial palaces, two monasteries, an arsenal, and a museum called the Treasury, where are preserved the coronation robes of every Czar and Czarina, the presents made to them on their accession to the throne, or their marriages, and a great variety of valuable articles possessed by them during their lives. It is one of the most remarkable and interesting collections in the world, and the worth of the jewels in the imperial crowns and fastened on the imperial mantles, and even on saddles and bridles, must be something extraordinary. The gowns worn by the Czarinas at their coronation are all there, with their gloves and even their shoes and stockings; and they show plainly that, since the time of the great Catherine, most of these imperial ladies have been of slender form, and have worn such small shoes that even a modern belle might be proud of them. The presents to the new Czar were also deposited there, and I noticed attentively the gift of the Mikado as well as that of the King of Corea. The Mikado's present is a peacock in ivory, of full natural size and most lively action, and wrought with such refinement that every feather in the bird's tail is a separate piece of ivory that may be taken out and put back again. The Corean King's gift is a large screen of porcelain, painted with extraordinary skill and delicacy, and apparently the work of Japanese artists, since the living Coreans cannot do that kind of thing.

The religious edifice in the Kremlin that one naturally enters first is the Church of the Assumption, in which the Czars are always crowned. Standing in the centre of the citadel, it has a very large dome, with a smaller dome at each of its four corners. These domes are covered with gold, as we were assured, not gilding. The interior is simple in its design, but filled with pictures and other ornaments. The space in the interior is small, so that the number of persons who can be admitted to witness the coronation of a Czar is inconveniently limited.

A religious edifice more interesting in itself is the Voznesenski or Ascension Convent, likewise in the Kremlin, containing two churches, one used for services in the winter and the other in the pleasant parts of the year. We went there one Sunday morning and found the church filled; and on this occasion, contrary to the usual custom in Russia, there were more women than men among the worshippers. The convent possesses an *eikon*, an image of the Virgin of Kazan, which is believed to be endowed with miraculous powers that are exercised especially in the cases of sick children. After the regular mass was completed, a number of women came up to the officiating priest, each carrying a child in her arms, and the priest, reciting a little prayer, held up the *eikon* to be kissed by the child, or to be touched. This ceremony lasted fully half an hour, and, as our party were standing watching the little creatures, as, one after the other, they were brought to the venerated image, our interpreter touched my elbow and pointed to a large dignified lady, perhaps fifty years old, in monastic costume, who was coming toward us, accompanied by two young nuns, from the other extremity of the church. "That is the Lady Abbess," said he, "and she seems to be coming to you." Immediately she arrived, and, holding out her hand, shook hands with me and with the ladies of the party, saying in Russian: "It is a great pleasure to see Americans, and I have come to tell you how glad we are that you visit our church." She had scarcely turned to go away when another lady, also large and dignified, and richly dressed in black, but not wearing a bonnet, approached from the other side of the church. "Why," said the interpreter, "that is the Grand Duchess! She lives in the monastery." And, sure enough, she had come on the same errand. She shook hands with each one of us in turn, and said that she could not resist the impulse to express her gratification at seeing Americans in Moscow. This was most pleasant, and we received the spontaneous greetings of the distinguished ladies with a deep patriotic satisfaction.

The next Sunday we went to the morning service in the Cathedral of the Saviour, a vast and magnificent structure in granite, commenced under the late Emperor Nicholas I. It stands near the Kremlin, on the west. The church was crowded, and in number the men very greatly exceeded the women. This, as I have said before, is the usual thing in Russia. The men appear to be more religious, more passionately devout, than the women, and any great occasion in the Church is likely to demonstrate this peculiarity. We entered very soon after the service had begun. The guide told me that about five thousand people were already assembled. There are no seats in the Russian churches, and we were standing in the crowd, very near a little inclosure which is found in every Russian church, where wax tapers are kept for the use of the worshippers. One enters and buys a taper, which he lights and sets up before the image of some saint, and then, bowing to the ground, performs his devotions. While we were there in the crowd, a large, elderly man who was posted inside the inclosure, bent forward to our guide: "Are not these Americans?" he asked in Russian. "Yes, sir," was the answer. "Will you say to the gentleman and the ladies that if they will come inside here, I can offer them seats?" We accepted most thankfully, and occupied the three chairs he gave us as the service proceeded. When it was completed, our hospitable friend arose and, reaching his hand to me, said: "Russia and America have always been friends." "Yes," I replied, "and, please God, they always will be!" As we went out of the inclosure to look through the interior of the church the guide whispered to me: "That is one of the great merchants of Moscow."

This leads me to recount a circumstance that illustrates a very amiable peculiarity of Russian character, namely, kindness and generosity toward strangers. It occurred at a previous visit to Moscow, but that makes no difference. Arriving at the railway station one morning after travelling all night, the compartment occupied by my party in the carriage was suddenly invaded by a number of hotel porters. Seizing the small articles of our luggage, they were going out with them, and I vainly appealed to them in German and in French to stop. While this contest was at its height a tall Russian gentleman in military uniform and wearing a sword came from the adjoining compartment and spoke to me in French. "I see that you are in some trouble," he said. "Will you kindly allow me to assist you?" I thanked him most heartily, while the porters subsided. Asking to what hotel we wished to go, he sent for the representative of that house, who was waiting near by in the station, committed us to his care, saw that our baggage and trunks were all safely packed in the carriage, and, when everything was completed, shook hands with me and turned away. I could hardly thank him sufficiently, especially as he had spent fully half an hour in this politeness to unknown strangers, who had no claim upon his attention. I afterward caused inquiries to be made, and ascertained that he was an officer of very high rank and distinction; and I mention the circumstance here because it corresponds with all my observations elsewhere as to the goodness of the Russian people. They are the most kind-hearted people in the world. It is impossible to exaggerate their benevolence toward strangers, no matter who they may be. As I thought it over there on the spot, I was ashamed of myself; for I could not imagine devoting a whole half hour to the service of three or four unknown foreigners at the Grand Central Station, for instance, merely because they had got into a dispute with a lot of hotel porters. But the spontaneous kindness of a Russian, no matter in what station of life, I have never seen appealed to in vain.

Another church which every one should visit and study in Moscow is the Cathedral of St. Basil in the Red Square, near the southeast corner of the Kremlin. It was begun about 1550 and finished before the end of the sixteenth century. It is very irregular in its design, has eleven domes of different forms, and contains in the interior eleven different chapels. It is impossible to describe the wonderful effect of color which it exhibits. The domes are painted, each with its own pigments, and in the lapse of ages the original hues have taken on an indescribable softness that gives to the whole structure a charm nobody can imagine who has not seen it. I tried to get a photograph that would reproduce in some degree, or even suggest the special qualities of these colors; but it was in vain. Photographs are abundant enough, but they are all in bright and crude tones that make them almost caricatures, and suggest nothing of the amazing poetry which converts this church into one of the most original and beautiful buildings that any architect has ever designed. There is a legend that when it was finished Ivan the Terrible, who was then the Czar, put out the eyes of the architect, so that another like it might never be built. This is not a true story, and one can take pleasure in diminishing the list of cruelties attributed to Ivan; but, considering the strangeness and the fascination of the church, it would have been a natural desire in him to prevent the creation of another like it.

Another sacred edifice which one cannot help visiting is the little Iverskaia, or Iberian chapel, standing in the middle of the gateway and of the street at the entrance to the Red Square, near the northeast corner of the Kremlin. The street here divides, with ample room for carriages on either side. At the open door of the chapel there is always a crowd of pious worshippers, and no one, except perhaps some hopeless Anarchist, ever passes by without crossing himself, or at least raising his hat, in token of sympathy, if not of reverence. The Czar always goes first to this chapel when he arrives in Moscow, before entering the Kremlin or setting foot in his own house. The *eikon* which gives this peculiar interest to the place is a copy of the Virgin of Mount Athos, made in 1648, and bearing upon the right cheek a scratch given by the sword of a Tartar. This sacred image is very often carried through the streets for the benefit of some sick person. It is borne habitually in a carriage with six horses, and is followed by a long procession of ecclesiastics chanting and saying prayers, while the people pause on the sidewalks, many of them kneeling, and carriages and horses are excluded from the streets.

Besides the places we have mentioned, there are a thousand in and about Moscow that the foreigner would wish to visit; but there are two especially which he ought not to miss. One of these is the Romanoff house, the original city residence of the family whose descendants have ruled Russia now for nearly three hundred years. It is a solid stone building with fifty odd feet of frontage, and was burned out by the French, but has since been restored with historical accuracy. On the street it is one story high, and in the courtyard four stories, and it has been arranged to represent the mode of life usual in noble Russian families in the Middle Ages. The entrance is through the courtyard, and the visitor is allowed to go through the whole edifice and to inspect the furniture and the domestic arrangements in every department.

But far more attractive to the imagination than this ancient abode of the Romanoffs is the house where Napoleon slept the night before he entered Moscow at the head of his army, an event followed by the disastrous retreat from Russia, which opened the path to Waterloo and St. Helena. It stands on an elevation known as the Sparrow Hills, about five miles' drive from the Kremlin. A railroad also takes passengers to the place. The hills are high enough to afford a superb view of the city. The house occupied by Napoleon is small, but the vista that he had, with the line of march of his army directly beneath his eye, was magnificent. The march was across the broad and level intervale of the little river Moskva, with the Kremlin as its objective point. And so the third act in the most showy tragedy of the nineteenth century was completed; and who knows whether or no there will be other such tragedies in the twentieth?

From Moscow to Warsaw is about eight hundred and twenty miles through an agricultural country, with villages built to lodge the agricultural farm laborers, and with forests covering more land than is cultivated. It is a rather commonplace region in itself, but the travelling is quite delightful. There is no hurry, the stops are frequent enough, the tea is always good, and the pervading peace of the landscape is most restful. There is no line to mark the difference between the country on the two sides of the frontier; yet there is a charm, an indescribable something, a gentle poesy that seems to dwell over the Polish farms and chateaux, and is somehow wanting on the Russian side. This charm continues as the journey ends and you are in Warsaw.

This ancient capital of Poland I should call the most poetic city in Europe. Its situation is exceedingly beautiful. There are neither very high hills nor very deep valleys, but the low land is on the north of the Vistula and the high land on the south of it, and in fact the diversification everywhere is picturesque to the last degree and keeps the imagination busy at every turn. There are plenty of interesting buildings in Warsaw, both ancient and modern. To one that is just out of the city I made two studious visits, and this was the old chateau of John Sobieski, built by that famous warrior after his campaigns against the Turks were done, and he had come back to Poland loaded with spoils and with the gratitude of Vienna and of Austria, which he had saved from being added to the Turkish dominions.

The Sobieski house now belongs to the Countess Potocka, if she is still living; if not, I suppose it has gone to her son, Count Potocki, a graceful and handsome young fellow of genuine Polish beauty, who is thirty odd years old, and is known among his friends as the richest man in Poland. It is a spacious country house, an Italian villa in form, its wings on either side crowded with objects of art, with old armor, with pictures, and with historical souvenirs of every nature. A portrait of the original Countess Potocka, a Circassian lady who came to Poland by way of Turkey, and whose romantic tale is the glory of many novels, is one of the pictures, showing that her loveliness was not merely an effect of features and complexion, but of wit and intelligence as well.

In driving back to the city we passed into the Lazienski park, and went through the palace built by King Stanislas Poniatowski, and bought by Czar Alexander I, eighty years ago. A more charming house, or one more beautifully decorated, cannot be found. The park which surrounds it is very admirable, and the whole establishment can crow loud and high over the general ruck of royal chateaux in the other countries of Europe.

I spent an afternoon in the Jewish quarter of the city, and came away full of admiration for the energy, business faculty, and apparent prosperity of the respected Semites. Warsaw contains about five hundred thousand people, and one third of them are Jews. As men of business, they are shrewd, energetic, judicious, and successful; as scholars, they are learned, profound, accurate, and indefatigable; as men of religion, they adhere conscientiously and faithfully to the doctrine of their fathers. The quarter of the city which they occupy is certainly not the most beautiful, but it is reasonably clean and wonderfully industrious. There is progress in them.

But it is time to turn our faces toward the West. A brief railway ride to Berlin and Bremen brings us to the steamer, and after a few days on the steamer we are at home again. Our summer journey has lasted a little less than three months, all without a single mishap, or even a day of stormy weather. It has shown us some of the most interesting things in the world; but what part of this mundane sphere is better than Long Island, with the waters of the Sound breaking gently upon its beaches, and the Stars and Stripes keeping guard over all?

VIII.

HOW TO GET TO JERUSALEM.

EVERY Christian and every philosophic student of history must desire to see Jerusalem. It was formerly very difficult and even dangerous to go there. But now it is safe, easy, and comparatively inexpensive.

There are various roads for the traveller to choose from. He may start from Egypt and follow the route through the desert of Sinai; or he may land at Beirut, in Central Syria, pass the hills of Lebanon, and proceed southward through the country of Galilee; but each of these routes involves a long journey on horseback, with a caravan and tents and guards. The simplest and shortest way is through Jaffa, or Joppa, as it was called in St. Paul's time. This is the seaport in the

Eastern Mediterranean that is nearest to Jerusalem; and a railway, finished in 1893, bears the traveller directly to his destination. From Constantinople steamers for Jaffa are frequent, and so they are from Alexandria and Port Said, the nearest Egyptian ports. But landing at Jaffa is uncertain. It is an open roadstead, not a sheltered harbor; and between the anchoring ground of ships and the beach there stretches a long and sharp-edged reef, just rising to the surface of the water; and on a windy day the breakers falling upon it are shattered into foam. In this reef there is a narrow passage, wide enough for a whaleboat; and once through, there is safety. But the slightest variation from the true line hurls your boat upon the rocks and drowns its passengers. Just before we were there in November a boat's crew had been destoyed; and usually, if a westerly wind is blowing, steamers will not attempt to land, but carry away the pilgrims to a more distant port and an uncertain destination. But with the increased traffic of Jaffa, it cannot, we suppose, be very long before a safe harbor is built there, and the debarkation of voyagers made safe and comfortable.

After you are well ashore at Jaffa, you have two good ways of reaching Jerusalem. First there is the old carriage road, which has existed for many years, and a very good road it is; and then there is the new railroad. The carriage road is shorter than the railroad, being something like thirty-two miles long, while the railroad is some fifty miles; but it takes twice as much time to get there with a carriage and horses, and it is, of course, much more costly. The railroad is very good indeed, substantially built by French engineers with French capital, though the locomotives which I noticed bore the mark of a Philadelphia firm. For some twenty miles the line passes through the fertile and attractive plain of Sharon, that rich and lovely ancient region whose verdant beauty wars and devastations have not extinguished. Then it enters the mountains and follows the lines of small streams, and during the remainder of the distance winds about through ravines, especially the Wady Surar and the Wady Bittir. The ascent from the sea to Jerusalem amounts to two thousand four hundred and eighty feet in all. I saw no indications of great difficulties overcome in the engineering. There may be a tunnel or two, though I do not remember any distinctly. The trains that were running consisted of two second-class carriages and one first-class. These carriages are divided into compartments much like the cars of the Swiss and Italian railways. The first-class seats are not cushioned, but are just like our ordinary cane-seated chairs. There was one daily train that made the round trip between Jaffa and Jerusalem, and the first-class fare was ten francs. The time of leaving Jerusalem was 9 A. M., and the returning train started from Jaffa at 2 P. M. The running time is about three hours and a half. The language used upon the line by guards and station men is French.

I have been told by my friend, Dr. Pereira Mendes, that there is a notion among Oriental Jews that the opening of a railway to Jerusalem must precede the coming of the Messiah. This he heard nearly twenty years ago when minister of a congregation almost wholly composed of Hebrews from northern Africa, Turkey, Greece, Asia Minor, and the farther East. The foundation for the opinion appears to be the last chapter of the prophecies of Isaiah, in an eloquent prediction of the return of the Hebrew exiles, where we read: "They shall bring all your brethren out of all the nations, for an offering unto the Lord, upon horses, and in chariots, and in litters, and upon mules, and upon swift beasts to my holy mountain Jerusalem, saith the Lord."

The Hebrew word which is translated "swift beasts" in the English version is כרכרות (kirkaroth), and occurs only this once in all the Bible. The roots of the word are found in 2 Samuel, vi, 14, where it is applied to the swaying dance of David, and is the common Hebrew word for furnace. Hence the derived meaning, as Dr. Mendes tells me, "a swaying furnace." For the English rendering there is no justification whatever in the sense of the Hebrew word in the text. Some propose to translate it "dromedaries"; but the same prophet only a few chapters before (lx, 6), uses a totally different word, the accepted equivalent of which is "dromedary." It is certainly neither camels nor asses, for there are well-known Hebrew words regularly used for these. When the English translation was made in King James's time there was no word to express the Hebrew in this passage; but what more accurate epithet could be applied to a railway locomotive than to call it a swaying furnace? And what more accurate term could the prophet use to describe what he had seen in his vision of the return of the Hebrews by all kinds of conveyances, among them one which he had never beheld in all his experience, but which "swayed" and carried fire? What a picturesque word to describe a train or locomotive in rapid motion!

In passing through the mountains between the plain of Sharon and Jerusalem the scenery is fine and interesting, though nowhere very extraordinary. In November the mountains were generally red and bare, though wherever there was moisture the grass was green, and the olive trees still bore their foliage. There are frequent terraces also along the sides of the hills, and vineyards are planted there. In a good season there ought to be a good crop of wine in the country. But it is not a fertile country by any means, any more than it was in the days when Abram was obliged by bad crops and short supplies to go down to Egypt to escape starving.

The thoughts and emotions which naturally belong to one's arrival at a spot which has played in the history of mankind a part so tremendous, are not much promoted when we reach the Jerusalem Railway terminus and take in the spectacle which opens upon our eyes. As we gaze around, nothing that we see produces the effect either of antiquity or of sacredness. The station buildings are new, and we see new buildings, both finished and unfinished, with various evidences of modern activity and progress, upon almost every height that rises in the range of vision. All is noise, bustle, and confusion; and the traveller may even be stirred with fear for his personal safety in the disputes of cab drivers and hotel agents for the possession of his person and luggage.

The terminus is about a mile from the

principal western gate, known as the Jaffa gate, which leads through the walls into the ancient city. I have seen it alleged in some newspaper that the terminus is in the valley of Hinnom, but it is a mistake. The valley of Hinnom bounds the western and southern lines of the city wall; but between it and the railway there is a ridge of land; and as we cross it in driving toward the town, we look down into that part of the valley where of old the pious King Josiah "defiled Tophet, which is in the valley of the children of Hinnom, that no man might make his son or his daughter to pass through the fire to Moloch;" and where long afterward, as Jeremiah records, the heaven-defying children of Judah "built the high places of Baal, which are in the valley of the son of Hinnom, to cause their sons and their daughters to pass through the fire unto Moloch."

As we leave this ill-famed ravine and turn toward the east, the lofty wall of

Jerusalem and the massive towers of the citadel are immediately before us. We are on the outer slope of Mount Zion, the sanctuary and the abode of David! The ponderous blocks which form the lower strata of the wall might have been shaped and put in place by some prehistoric race of giants. More than almost anything else to be found around Jerusalem, or within, this wall bears an appearance of great antiquity. We can easily believe that its foundations were laid in the time of David, though its upper portions are unquestionably modern. The books vary. One says it was the work of Sultan Suleiman in the sixteenth century; another that it was erected much earlier; and my guide, a most intelligent and well-informed Jew of Hungarian origin, told me it was built by the Crusaders after they had got possession, for the purpose of protecting the inhabitants against the rascally Arabs, who would ride up in small parties, rob some rich family, and be off with their plunder before anything could be done to stop them. But, however this may be, the wall, from sixteen to twenty feet in height, fully encloses the town; and, although it could soon be knocked to pieces by a ten-pounder cannon, it stands in good order, solid enough for all peaceful purposes, and perfectly separates the city from the country about it.

While you are gazing at the old wall, your carriage moves along, and presently you find yourself stepping out at the door of your hotel, and it is on Mount Zion!

> Beautiful in elevation, the joy of the whole earth,
> Is Mount Zion, on the sides of the north,
> The city of the great King!
> Walk about Zion, and go round about her;
> Tell the towers thereof.
> Mark well her bulwarks,
> Consider her palaces:
> That ye may tell it to the generation following.
> For this God is our God forever and ever;
> He will be our guide even unto death!

IX.

THE HOLY CITY.

As we get a complete view of Jerusalem and begin to understand it, the first impression is surprise at its evident prosperity, due, as we presently understand, to the sums of money spent by the great and increasing mass of pilgrims who habitually resort there; and then we are even more surprised at the smallness of the place. It can never have been what would be called a large town; and Dr. W. M. Thomson, the author of "The Land and the Book," who examined the question very carefully some fifteen years ago, is convinced that in the time of its greatest glory it was never much larger than it is now. The actual present length of the wall which encloses the city, according to Dr. Thomson, is about two miles and a half, measuring the whole of the four sides; and the greatest length which he attributes to it in ancient times is a mile and a half from north to south, with an average breadth of half a mile from west to east, making the enclosed area something like two hundred and ten or two hundred and fifteen acres. Josephus also gives the total measurement of the walls before their destruction by Titus at thirty-three furlongs, or a little over four miles. Roughly speaking, then, Jerusalem in its highest splendor was not larger than the area of the Central Park below the reservoir. Moreover, this limited space has always been diminished by the extent of the area levelled and walled, set apart of old for the Temple, and still held sacred by the Turkish authorities against the erection of ordinary buildings. This area contains, I should suppose, from thirty to thirty-five acres. It is the one conspicuous green spot in Jerusalem. It is covered with grass and adorned with trees; and the only buildings on it are the glorious and beautiful Mosque of Omar, the Mosque of Aksa, and one or two other dependent structures.

The present population of Jerusalem is not far from forty thousand, and more than half are Jews. They live in a separate quarter of their own, as do also the various divisions of Christians, such as the Armenians, the Greeks, and the Protestants. All these quarters are densely built, with narrow and irregular lanes for streets, but the prevailing prosperity does not seem to reach the abodes of the Hebrews. The indications are all of extreme poverty. A synagogue was pointed out bearing an inscription showing that it was the gift of a Paris Rothschild; but its mean appearance and unattractive surroundings bore no suggestion of critical refinement in the congregation. The articles of food set out for sale in the petty little shops were often squalid and repulsive. We came so often upon spoiled salt fish among the stores exposed by the venders, that we concluded it must form a regular element of diet in the quarter. There was no visible sign of industry by which the people might earn their living; and no one need be surprised to learn that in various parts of the world the well-to-do and charitable Jews are regularly called upon to contribute to the support of their pauper brethren in Jerusalem.

We hate to say a word that may discourage any one's search after knowledge; but we must advise our readers who are preparing to see Jerusalem not to read too many books of modern exploration and criticism, for fear of losing all faith in the holy places where the remembrance of the founder of the Christian religion is most religiously preserved. This modern criticism, conducted in considerable part by men as pious as they are learned, has put into dispute almost every spot of importance in the history of the sacred city. Excepting the site of the Temple and the Mount of Olives, I don't think there is a single locality which remains free from question or denial. The place of the crucifixion and burial of Christ, as the great body of Christians have believed for fifteen hundred years, is marked by the Church of the Holy Sepulchre; but, apart from the Roman Catholics, the orthodox Greeks, and the Armenians, the majority of Christians would seem to have fixed their faith upon a quite different quarter outside of the present city wall. It is true that few scholars express themselves upon this subject with the vehemence employed by the late Mr. Laurence Oliphant. He avers that "it has now been proved to a demonstration that wherever the tomb in which Christ was laid after his crucifixion may have been, it could not have been in the cave over which the gorgeous edifice called the Church of the Holy

Sepulchre now stands." The same writer declares that "the Jerusalem of the present day, the holy city of the world *par excellence*, contains within its walls more sacred shams and impostures than any other city in the world."

It is evident that much study in this direction cannot lead to that reverential and prayerful spirit in which any person of Christian education must naturally approach the place where he believes the Redeemer of the world was laid after his execution ; and we turn with pleasure from such skepticism to the opposing utterance of such an authority as Mr. William C. Prime. He is a Protestant, understands the question thoroughly, and is familiar with the views of all the scholars who have written upon the subject: yet he believes in the genuineness of the Holy Sepulchre. "Critical scholars and learned men employed in investigating the topography of the Holy Land," writes Mr. Prime, "had no doubt of its authenticity in the beginning of the fourth century; no one, so far as we know, thought in that age of disputing the fact, but all men acknowledged its truth; it is not doubted by any one that this is the locality in which those learned men placed their confidence, it having been well preserved from that time to this."

But, whatever the attitude of the mind toward these questions, it is impossible without deep emotion to observe the throngs of pilgrims from east or west that daily visit the Church of the Holy Sepulchre. We were there one morning when a company of Russians, several hundred in number, as we were told, came to make their devotions at the shrine. They were humble people, men, women, and youths; but the intensity and sincerity of their feeling, as they prostrated themselves to kiss the stone pavement in front of the sepulchre, no language could exaggerate. The canker of doubt and the infection of irreverence had never touched their honest and faithful souls. How much more enviable they appeared there in their devout prostration than the skeptic who contemns and the scoffer who jeers at their simple, unquestioning belief!

The Church of the Holy Sepulchre was first built by the Empress Helena, the mother of Constantine the Great, in the first half of the fourth century. Two hundred years later it was burned by the Persians, but was soon built up again. In the tenth century it was twice badly damaged by fire, and in the beginning of the eleventh century it was injured and desecrated by the Mohammedans. Finally in the twelfth century the Crusaders restored it; and, although it has been repeatedly injured by hostile attacks and by accidental conflagrations, much of the original features is still preserved. Around it and opening into it the Catholics, the orthodox Greeks, the Armenians, and the Copts have chapels of their own;

and of these that of the Greeks is by far the most ornate and magnificent. To its own chapel each one of these parties has, of course, an exclusive right; but the use of the central church for religious services is allotted to each in its order, and for a certain time of the day; and a guard of Turkish soldiers is constantly present within the outer door of the church to enforce this order and to keep the different kinds of Christians from disturbing the public peace by contentions for unregulated possession of the church.

The Chapel of the Holy Sepulchre is a small structure of polished stone in the rotunda of the church, under the high vault of its roof. Fifteen lamps are kept burning in this chapel: five belonging to the Greeks, five to the Catholics, four to the Armenians, and one to the Copts. The sarcophagus in which the Lord is believed to have rested, is fitted with a cover of polished stone, porphyry, I think, and this covering is believed by most visitors to be the sepulchre itself. It is constantly worn away by the kisses of the faithful, and has to be replaced every few years. The same is the case with the manger at Bethlehem, where, as the Gospel tells us, Christ was laid as an infant; and that, too, lasts but a little time, so fervent and so constant are the kisses which pious believers hasten to bestow upon it.

Near the chapel of the sepulchre, and within the enclosure of the church, the visitor is also permitted to examine the place where Christ was nailed to the cross, and the socket in the rock where the cross was erected. Close by in another chapel is the place where the vestments of Christ were divided; another chapel is said to stand over the spot where the crown of thorns was put upon Him; and in another the impress of His feet is shown in the stone. The skeptic will not admit that these things are true, or that there is any sanctity in the places that inspire the believer with awe and wonder. But for the pious pilgrim, what subjects of religious meditation and holy ecstasy are offered in such relics and such traces of the Saviour's very footsteps! No wonder that the whole Christian world is drawn to Jerusalem by tens of thousands.

The criticism which denies the genuineness of all these remains and relics in and around the Church of the Holy Sepulchre rests upon the argument that this part of Jerusalem was included within the walls of the city at the time of the crucifixion, and that, accordingly, Christ could not have been put to death there, since it is certain that the place of execution was without the wall. The same argument would overthrow the belief, which has also prevailed for centuries, that it was through the street known as the Via Dolorosa that the Divine Victim was led from the tribunal of Pilate to the place of death. This street is perhaps half a mile long, and it is everywhere in close proximity to the present outer wall. Fourteen stations marked with tablets appear to show the path followed from the place of condemnation to the place of execution; and of these, seven or eight are in the Via Dolorosa. At one of them the cross was laid upon the shoulders of Jesus; another is at the spot where he is said to have fallen under that burden; at another he met his mother; at another Simon of Cyrene took the cross from him; at another he paused to speak to the women who accompanied the procession; and at another it is said that he fell again. The last five stations are in the church and the various chapels.

But, if it be true, as the so-called higher critics now maintain, that the crucifixion took place, not on the site now marked by the Holy Sepulchre, but on a hill at a short distance outside of the Damascus Gate, it must follow that the Via Dolorosa and its stations cannot have been the line of march which was followed on that tremendous day. We shall not attempt to consider this controversy at any length, much less to express a decision respecting it. It is enough for our purpose to say that for fifteen hundred years the Christian Church almost unanimously adhered to this belief, and that to reject it would be to change Jerusalem from a home and centre of unquestioning faith into a theatre of disputation and uncertainty.

Turning from the Via Dolorosa and entering into a street broad enough for a carriage, which leads across the city toward the south, we come to a high-vaulted passage two or three hundred feet long, with shops on each side of it, through which we proceed to the stairs that ascend to the ancient platform of the Temple. It was out of this entrance, as the tradition tells us, that "He cast out all them that sold and bought in the Temple, and overthrew the tables of the money changers and the seats of them that sold doves; and he saith unto them. 'It is written, my house shall be called a house of prayer, but ye make it a den of robbers.'"

A few steps and we mount to the open place where the Temple formerly stood. It is perhaps ten feet higher than the level of the city on the west; and on the east a substantial wall separates it from the Valley of Kedron, beyond which we behold the trees of Gethsemane and the Mount of Olives. On the south a much more massive wall, which completes the quadrangle toward the Valley of Jehoshaphat and Hinnom, is undoubtedly a remnant of the foundations which sustained the Temple of Herod; and a considerable portion of it may even date from the Temple of Solomon.

As we have already said, the principal structure which stands upon this historic plateau, is the Mosque of Omar, named after the first Moslem conqueror of Jerusalem, although it is far from certain that he was concerned in building it. But, at any rate, it is one of the most sacred places known to the Mohammedan religion. It is second in sanctity only to the Mosque of the Kaaba in Mecca itself. More than this, it is one of the most beautiful among religious edifices, not from its magnitude or from any peculiar genius in its construction, but from the extraordinary charm of its decoration within and without. It is in the shape of an octagon, with each side measuring sixty-six feet long. The outer walls are divided by a moulding or cornice which separates them into a basement sixteen feet high covered with marble, and an upper story twenty feet high, covered entirely with Persian tiles of many colors, most delicate patterns, and splendid lustre, producing altogether an effect of surprising fascination. Nothing could be compared to it, except perhaps a gigantic kaleidoscope displaying an endless succession of gorgeous gems and dazzling brilliancy. When you stand near enough to distinguish the tints and the patterns of the tiles, you are absorbed in a delight such as you never felt elsewhere; and if you stand too far off to see so minutely, the effect is that of an infinitely soft and ever-varying rainbow.

Yet there is no uniformity in the patterns or colors of the tiles, though the whole of each panel is covered with the same color and the same pattern. The tiles themselves are in the very highest style of Persian art, made, I should suppose, not later than the thirteenth or fourteenth century, when this branch of keramics was carried to a perfection and a splendor in Persia that have not been attained elsewhere. Accordingly, this part of the mosque must have been decorated some eight or nine hundred years after the structure of the building had been completed, if indeed we may say that it is completed yet. When we were there we saw men at work putting up over the tiles which adorn the outer wall a frieze of other tiles, likewise Persian, each of them two feet or thereabouts in height, of an indigo-blue lustre, and bearing raised white Arabic letters, also about two feet high, and so plain that they could be read easily from some distance below, setting forth verses from the Koran adoring and praising the Most High. This frieze was not yet finished as much as half way around the octagon at the time when we inspected it, and it looked as if it formed a part of the original design, which they just now had the means to execute. When it is done it will add very greatly to the dignity and solemnity of the mosque.

The interior of this famous house of worship bore to the full that appearance of high prosperity which we had noticed elsewhere in Jerusalem. The mosaics which beautify the roof seemed almost as brilliant as those of St. Mark's itself, though far less elaborate. The cleanness of the house was perfect, and every inch of the floor was carpeted with rugs of exquisite taste and richness. When the priests came forward to welcome us within the doors we could tell them without exaggeration that we did not know, even in Christendom, another temple of religion more faultless in itself, more worthily cared for, or more beautifully maintained.

In the centre of the mosque stands the Holy Rock, the one thing in Jerusalem about whose antiquity and identity controversy seems almost impossible. The traditions attached to it are innumerable. Abraham and Melchizedek sacrificed burnt offerings upon it; it was here that Abraham was prevented by the angel from killing his son Isaac; here David established the ark of the covenant; here above the rock was raised the altar of burnt offering in the Temple of Solomon; here, according to the Moslem tradition, was written the unspeakable name of

God, which Jesus alone was able to read; hence Mohammed ascended to heaven; at the Last Day the Kaaba from Mecca will be brought here, and then the final trump will sound, and the dead will be brought to judgment. The rock is of irregular natural form. It is more than fifty feet long and forty feet wide, and channels are shown in it through which the blood of the sacrifices is said to have flowed away. How David became possessor of the place is recorded in the Second Book of Samuel.

"And God came back that day to David and said: 'Go up and rear an altar unto the Lord in the threshing floor of Araunah, the Jebusite.' And David, according to the saying of God, went up as the Lord commanded. And Araunah looked and saw the King and his servants coming toward him; and Araunah went out and bowed himself before the King on his face upon the ground. And Araunah said: 'Wherefore is my Lord, the King, come to his servant?' And David said: 'To buy the threshing floor of thee, to build an altar unto the Lord that the plague may be stayed from the people.' And Araunah said unto David: 'Let my Lord, the King, take and offer up what seemeth good unto him. Behold the oxen for the burnt offering, and the threshing instruments and the furniture of the oxen for the wood; and all these, O King, doth Araunah give unto the king.' And Araunah said unto the King, 'The Lord, thy God, accept thee.' And the King said unto Araunah: 'Nay, but I will verily buy it of thee at a price. Neither will I offer burnt offerings unto the Lord my God which cost me nothing.' So David bought the threshing plough and the oxen for fifty shekels of silver. And David built there an altar unto the Lord and offered burnt offerings and peace offerings. So the Lord was entreated for the land, and the plague was stayed from Israel."

X.

BETHLEHEM AND BETHANY.

BETHLEHEM, revered of all Christians as the birthplace of the Saviour, lies six miles west of the citadel of Jerusalem; and Bethany, where He loved to withdraw from the crowd, and find rest in the society of near friends and disciples, lies about two miles to the east. The most hasty stay in the Holy City must include a visit to each of these places.

The road to Bethlehem is smooth and pleasant, and objects of extraordinary association approach the mind at every turn. Toward the southwest we behold the sunny fields which formed the scene of the lovely idyl of Ruth and Boaz, the most charming story of Hebrew literature. In the same direction is the Cave of Adullam, where

David, fighting man and captain but not yet King, had a refuge while the Philistines held his native town; and we know that toward the northwest, though invisible to us as yet, lies the valley where tradition tells us is the very field in which the shepherds were "keeping watch by night over their flock. And an angel of the Lord stood by them, and the glory of the Lord shone round about them; and they were sore afraid. And the angel said unto them: 'Be not afraid; for behold I bring you good tidings of great joy, which shall be to all the people; for behold, there is born to you this day in the city of David a Saviour which is Christ the Lord.'"

As we drive quietly along, the road passes almost within touching distance of "Rachel's sepulchre in the border of Benjamin at Zelzah," and we stop to gaze at the monument where the mother of Israel was laid to rest four thousand years ago. It is no longer in decay, having been repaired and made clean and seemly through the liberality of the late Moses Montefiore, of London. Christians, Jews, and Mohammedans all agree in venerating the mediæval structure, which stands here in the place of the pillar or pyramid of twelve rude stones corresponding to the twelve tribes of Israel, that marked the spot in the most ancient times. Wilson says that no doubt has ever been raised respecting this grave; yet as we open our Baedeker beside it, we read that "upon many grounds it is impossible" that Rachel can have been buried here!

Bethlehem is a very picturesque hill town. Thirty years ago the most intelligent visitors estimated its population at three thousand, but now our careful Baedeker puts it down at eight thousand, with scarcely any Mohammedans among them. It has shared the activity and the progress which have visited this entire region. The houses are uniformly of stone, and when we sought to approach the Great Church of the Nativity, we found the principal streets torn up in the process of laying down sewers, and were obliged to get down and go on foot. The church is a vast and complicated pile of buildings, the Latins and the Armenians having constructed chapels and monasteries about the original edifice, which is in the hands of the orthodox Greek communion. Here, as in Jerusalem, a guard of Turkish soldiers constantly attends in the entrance of the church to keep the disagreeing sorts of Christians out of violent quarrels with each other. The church dates back to the first half of the fourth century. The architecture of the interior is simple, severe, and most impressive; but some of the attached chapels are crowded with crucifixes, lamps of gold and silver, pictures and tapestries that bewilder the eye with their variety and splendor.

With lighted tapers in our hands, we descended to the Chapel of the Nativity. It was originally a cave, and a staircase of perhaps fifteen steps leads down to it. As we entered, we found the chapel occupied by the vesper service of a brotherhood of Franciscan monks. The Superior, a majestic old man, was officiating at the altar, and the fraternity, men of all ages, knelt upon the marble floor. The music they sang was noble, and the spirit of devotion that filled the scene was irresistible. Fortunate, indeed, are the pilgrims whose few hours in Bethlehem are made memorable by an accident so delightful, as was our presence at the vespers of the good Franciscans.

While Bethlehem more than met our expectation, Bethany rather proved a disappointment. It is an insignificant and decaying little hamlet, lying on the eastern slope of the Mount of Olives, and its few hundred people are all Moslems. To go there, the most convenient method is to drive from Jerusalem. After you reach the points known as the grave of Lazarus and the house of Mary and Martha, you leave the carriage, and make the rest of the journey over the Mount of Olives on donkeys. At the western foot of the Mount you visit the Garden of Gethsemane; and then you take your carriage again to return to the city.

While we know that Bethany was a favorite place of retirement with Jesus, there is no evidence to convince us that one or the other of the two places pointed out by popular tradition, and by the guides who conduct strangers, was habitually resorted to by Him: and no religious communion has adopted either of them as sacred and authentic. Yet as a whole Bethany is indisputably connected with many of the most intimate and impressive occurrences of the Gospel history; and as we pass slowly up its winding and neglected alleys upon our donkeys, with the height of the Mount before us and the clear autumn sky of Syria above, the mind is irresistibly carried back through the nineteen centuries; and the persons and events of the ancient days seem to the fancy, and almost to the eye, to be there again all real and living.

And so we move forward to the great Russian church on the summit, with the wonderful outlook from its porch upon the distant valley of the Jordan, and the blue strip of the Dead Sea which it reveals, and, beyond, all the mountains of Moab, with the peak of Nebo, whence Moses beheld the Promised Land which he might never enter. And then, mounting our donkeys again, we go down the western slope. There Jerusalem is before us and the mountains of Ephraim that close in the panorama upon the west, while at the foot is the garden of Gethsemane with its bowed and venerable cypresses whose age is counted by thousands of years; and there is the gentle and engaging old Italian monk who tends its flower beds and binds up packages of seeds for strangers to carry away. And as he receives the *douceur* that is reached toward him, "It is for the poor," he says; "it is not given in payment."

In all the world there is no other spot that so affects the thoughts of the visitor, nor any human narrative that can touch the heart with such infinite pathos as this of the Evangelist: "And they come unto a place which was named Gethsemane: and he saith unto his disciples, 'Sit ye here, while I pray.' And he taketh with him Peter and James and John, and began to be greatly amazed, and sore troubled. And he saith unto them, 'My soul is exceeding sorrowful even unto death; abide ye here, and watch.' And he went forward a little, and fell on the ground, and prayed that, if it were possible, the hour might pass away from him. And he said, 'Abba, Father, all things are possible unto thee; remove this cup from me: howbeit, not what I will, but what thou wilt.' And he cometh and findeth them sleeping and saith unto Peter: 'Simon, sleepest thou? Couldst thou not watch one hour? Watch and pray, that ye enter not into temptation: The spirit, indeed, is willing, but the flesh is weak.' And again he went away and prayed, saying the same words. And again he came, and found them sleeping, for their eyes were very heavy, and they wist not what to answer him. And he cometh the third time, and saith unto them, 'Sleep on now, and take your rest: it is enough, the hour is come; behold, the Son of man is betrayed into the hands of sinners. Arise, let us be going; behold, he that betrayeth me is at hand.'"

THE END.

D. APPLETON AND COMPANY'S PUBLICATIONS.

IN JOYFUL RUSSIA. By JOHN A. LOGAN, Jr. With 50 Illustrations in color and black and white. 12mo. Cloth, $3.50.

"Of extreme interest from beginning to end. Mr. Logan has animation of style, good spirits, a gift of agreeable and enlivening expression, and a certain charm which may be called companionableness. To travel with him must have been a particular pleasure. He has sense of humor, a way of getting over rough places, and understanding of human nature. There is not a dull chapter in his book."—*New York Times.*

"Mr. Logan has written of the things which he saw with a fullness that leaves nothing to be desired for their comprehension; with an eye that was quick to perceive their novelty, their picturesqueness, their national significance, and with a mind not made up beforehand—frankly open to new impressions, alert in its perceptions, reasonable in its judgment, manly, independent, and, like its environments, filled with holiday enthusiasm."—*New York Mail and Express.*

"No more fresh, original, and convincing picture of the Russian people and Russian life has appeared. . . . The author has described picturesquely and in much detail whatever he has touched upon. . . . Few books of travel are at once so readable and so informing, and not many are so successfully illustrated; for the pictures tell a story of their own, while they also interpret to the eye a vivid narrative."—*Boston Herald.*

"A chronicle of impressions gathered during a brief and thoroughly enjoyed holiday by a man with eyes wide open and senses alert to see and hear new things. Thoroughly successful and well worth perusal. . . . There will be found within its pages plenty to instruct and entertain the reader."—*Brooklyn Eagle.*

"The book is a historical novelty; and nowadays a more valuable distinction can not be attached to a book. . . . No other book of travels of late years is so unalterably interesting."—*Boston Journal.*

"Mr. Logan's narrative is spirited in tone and color. . . . A volume that is entertaining and amusing, and not unworthy to be called instructive. The style is at all times lively and spirited, and full of good humor."—*Philadelphia Press.*

"Mr. Logan has a quick eye, a ready pen, a determination to make the most of opportunities, and his book is very interesting. . . . He has made a thoroughly readable book in which history and biography are brought in to give one a good general impression of affairs."—*Hartford Post.*

"Mr. Logan has presented in attractive language, re-enforced by many beautiful photographs, a most entertaining narrative of his personal experiences, besides a dazzling panorama of the coronation ceremonies. . . . Read without prejudice on the subject of the Russian mode of government, the book is unusually able, instructive, and entertaining."—*Boston Globe.*

"Mr. Logan departs from the usual path, in telling in clear, simple, good style about the intimate life of the Russian people."—*Baltimore Sun.*

D. APPLETON AND COMPANY, NEW YORK.

D. APPLETON & CO.'S PUBLICATIONS.

A FRIEND OF THE QUEEN. (Marie Antoinette—Count de Fersen.) By PAUL GAULOT. With Two Portraits. 12mo. Cloth, $2.00.

"M. Gaulot deserves thanks for presenting the personal history of Count Fersen in a manner so evidently candid and unbiased."—*Philadelphia Bulletin.*

"There are some characters in history of whom we never seem to grow tired. Of no one is this so much the case as of the beautiful Marie Antoinette, and of that life which is at once so eventful and so tragic. . . . In this work we have much that up to the present time has been only vaguely known."—*Philadelphia Press.*

"A historical volume that will be eagerly read."—*New York Observer.*

"One of those captivating recitals of the romance of truth which are the gilding of the pill of history."—*London Daily News.*

"It tells with new and authentic details the romantic story of Count Fersen's (the Friend of the Queen) devotion to Marie Antoinette, of his share in the celebrated flight to Varennes, and in many other well-known episodes of the unhappy Queen's life."—*London Times.*

"If the book had no more recommendation than the mere fact that Marie Antoinette and Count Fersen are rescued at last from the voluminous and contradictory representations with which the literature of that period abounds, it would be enough compensation to any reader to become acquainted with the true delineations of two of the most romantically tragic personalities."—*Boston Globe.*

*T*HE ROMANCE OF AN EMPRESS. Catharine II of Russia. By K. WALISZEWSKI. With Portrait. 12mo. Cloth, $2.00.

"Of Catharine's marvelous career we have in this volume a sympathetic, learned, and picturesque narrative. No royal career, not even of some of the Roman or papal ones, has better shown us how truth can be stranger than fiction."—*New York Times.*

"A striking and able work, deserving of the highest praise."—*Philadelphia Ledger.*

"The book is well called a romance, for, although no legends are admitted in it, and the author has been at pains to present nothing but verified facts, the actual career of the subject was so abnormal and sensational as to seem to belong to fiction."—*New York Sun.*

"A dignified, handsome, indeed superb volume, and well worth careful reading."—*Chicago Herald.*

"It is a most wonderful story, charmingly told, with new material to sustain it, and a breadth and temperance and consideration that go far to soften one's estimate of one of the most extraordinary women of history."—*New York Commercial Advertiser.*

"The perusal of such a book can not fail to add to that breadth of view which is so essential to the student of universal history."—*Philadelphia Bulletin.*

New York: D. APPLETON & CO., 72 Fifth Avenue.

GERMANY AND THE GERMANS. By WILLIAM HARBUTT DAWSON, author of "German Socialism and Ferdinand Lassalle," "Prince Bismarck and State Socialism," etc. 2 vols., 8vo. Cloth, $6.00.

"This excellent work—a literary monument of intelligent and conscientious labor—deals with every phase and aspect of state and political activity, public and private, in the Fatherland. . . . Teems with entertaining anecdotes and introspective *aperçus* of character."—*London Telegraph.*

"With Mr. Dawson's two volumes before him, the ordinary reader may well dispense with the perusal of previous authorities. . . . His work, on the whole, is comprehensive, conscientious, and eminently fair."—*London Chronicle.*

"There is scarcely any phase of German national life unnoticed in his comprehensive survey. . . . Mr. Dawson has endeavored to write from the view-point of a sincere yet candid well-wisher, of an unprejudiced observer, who, even when he is unable to approve, speaks his mind in soberness and kindness."—*New York Sun.*

"'There is much in German character to admire; much in Germany's life and institutions from which Americans may learn. William Harbutt Dawson has succeeded in making this fact clearer, and his work will go far to help Americans and Germans to know each other better and to respect each other more. . . . It is a remarkable and a fascinating work."—*Chicago Evening Post.*

"One of the very best works on this subject which has been published up to date."—*New York Herald.*

A HISTORY OF GERMANY, *from the Earliest Times to the Present Day.* By BAYARD TAYLOR. With an Additional Chapter by MARIE HANSEN-TAYLOR. With Portrait and Maps. 12mo. Cloth, $1.50.

"There is, perhaps, no work of equal size in any language which gives a better view of the tortuous course of German history. Now that the story of a race is to be in good earnest a story of a nation as well, it begins, as every one, whether German or foreign, sees, to furnish unexpected and wonderful lessons. But these can only be understood in the light of the past. Taylor could end his work with the birth of the empire, but the additional narrative merely foreshadows the events of the future. It may be that all the doings of the past ages on German soil are but the introduction of what is to come. That is certainly the thought which grows upon one as he peruses this volume."—*New York Tribune.*

"When one considers the confused, complicated, and sporadic elements of German history, it seems scarcely possible to present a clear, continuous narrative. Yet this is what Bayard Taylor did. He omitted no episode of importance, and yet managed to preserve a main line of connection from century to century throughout the narrative."—*Philadelphia Ledger.*

"Probably the best work of its kind adapted for school purposes that can be had in English."—*Boston Herald.*

New York: D. APPLETON & CO., 72 Fifth Avenue.

D. APPLETON AND COMPANY'S PUBLICATIONS.

THE PRIVATE LIFE OF THE QUEEN. By a Member of the Royal Household. Illustrated. 12mo. Cloth, $1.50.

"The future historian will value 'The Private Life of the Queen' because it is in a sense so intimate. The contemporary reader will find it highly interesting for the same reason. . . . The book is agreeably written, and is certain to interest a very wide circle of readers."—*Philadelphia Press.*

"The author writes pleasantly, and the book is interesting in that it gives the reader a real acquaintance with the personality and private life of a singularly interesting public figure."—*New York Sun.*

"A singularly attractive picture of Queen Victoria. . . . The interests and occupations that make up the Queen's day, and the functions of many of the members of her household, are described in a manner calculated to gratify the natural desire to know what goes on behind closed doors that very few of the world's dignitaries are privileged to pass."—*Boston Herald.*

THE LIFE OF HIS ROYAL HIGHNESS THE PRINCE CONSORT. By Sir THEODORE MARTIN. In five volumes, each with Portrait. 12mo. Cloth, $10.00.

"The work bears the impress throughout of the directing mind of the Queen, and it is a very good reflex character—strong, even intense in her domestic affections, and yet with a decided taste and liking for public affairs and the duties of her position."—*The Interior.*

"A full and impartial biography of a noble and enlightened prince. . . . Mr. Martin's work is not gossipy, not light, nor yet dull, guarded in its details of the domestic lives of Albert and Victoria, but sufficiently full and familiar to contribute much interesting information. . . . Will well repay a careful and earnest reading."—*Chicago Tribune.*

"Although the work was prepared especially for English readers, it possesses universal interest, and will find a place in many private libraries on this side of the water."

THE SOVEREIGNS AND COURTS OF EUROPE. The Home and Court Life and Characteristics of the Reigning Families. By "POLITIKOS." With many Portraits. 12mo. Cloth, $1.50.

"A remarkably able book. . . . A great deal of the inner history of Europe is to be found in the work, and it is illustrated by admirable portraits."—*The Athenæum.*

"The anonymous author of these sketches of the reigning sovereigns of Europe appears to have gathered a good deal of curious information about their private lives, manners, and customs, and has certainly in several instances had access to unusual sources. The result is a volume which furnishes views of the kings and queens concerned, far fuller and more intimate than can be found elsewhere."—*New York Tribune.*

D. APPLETON AND COMPANY, NEW YORK.

D. APPLETON AND COMPANY'S PUBLICATIONS.

THE TRUE LIFE OF CAPTAIN SIR RICHARD F. BURTON. Written by his niece, GEORGIANA M. STISTED, with the authority and approval of the Burton family. 12mo. Cloth, with Portrait, $2.00.

"Miss Stisted has given us a thoroughly good biography. Though a great admirer of her uncle, she does not conceal his weaknesses, but writes, in the main, soberly and impartially with excellent judgment. She has compressed a great deal into a small volume, not confusing us with too much detail, and yet describing many picturesque incidents and scenes. Her book is interesting from beginning to end. Short as it is, we get from it a satisfactory idea of the story and personality of one of the most extraordinary men of his time."—*The Nation.*

"The book has not a dull line in it. Detail, anecdote, comment, and criticism are so nicely adjusted that the story never flags."—*Chicago Evening Post.*

"A very interesting biography of a very remarkable man."—*New York Mail and Express.*

THE EARLY CORRESPONDENCE OF HANS VON BÜLOW. Edited by his Widow. Selected and translated by CONSTANCE BACHE. With Portraits. 8vo. Cloth, $4.50.

"The book is valuable in furnishing an excellent insight into the musical history of the period, and to the astonishing standard which the musician had to attain before even recognition was assured by the extremely critical music-loving class of that time."—*San Francisco Argonaut.*

"As a mere story the book is extremely interesting, while as a psychological as well as a musical study the early life of Hans von Bülow, as mirrored forth in these letters, is of no small import."—*New York Mail and Express.*

"This volume introduces the Von Bülow not known to the present generation. The letters are free, spontaneous, and unstudied, exhibiting the musician struggling to make what he knew to be in him recognized by the public."—*London Daily Chronicle.*

GUSTAVE FLAUBERT, as seen in his Works and Correspondence. By JOHN CHARLES TARVER. With Portrait. 8vo. Buckram, $4.00.

"It is surprising that this extremely interesting correspondence has not been Englished before."—*London Athenæum.*

"This handsome volume is welcome. . . . It merits a cordial reception if for no other reason than to make a large section of the English public more intimately acquainted with the foremost champion of art for art's sake. . . . The letters are admirably translated, and in the main the book is written with skill and *verve*."—*London Academy.*

D. APPLETON AND COMPANY, NEW YORK.

D. APPLETON & CO.'S PUBLICATIONS.

AN AIDE-DE-CAMP OF NAPOLEON. Memoirs of General COUNT DE SÉGUR, of the French Academy, 1800-1812. Revised by his Grandson, COUNT LOUIS DE SÉGUR. 12mo. Cloth, $2.00.

"We say without hesitation that 'An Aide-de-Camp of Napoleon' is the book of memoirs above all others that should be read by those who are anxious to see Napoleon through the eyes of one of the many keen judges of character by whom he was surrounded."—*London Literary World.*

"The Count's personal story of adventure is so thrilling, and his opportunities of watching Napoleon were so constant and so ably utilized, that his work deserves honorable mention among works which show us history in the making, and the realities as well as the romance of war."—*London Daily Telegraph.*

"We thank the publishers for this translation of a most absorbing book. The story of Austerlitz is one involving so much genius that it must be read as a whole—all the good things with which the book abounds."—*London Daily Chronicle.*

"The historical interest is undoubtedly great. De Ségur's account of Napoleon's plans for the invasion of England is very interesting."—*London Times.*

"No recent work of which the present fashion for Napoleonic literature has witnessed either in the shape of translations from the French or of original monographs on his famous battles, is likely to interest a larger class of intelligent readers than 'An Aide-de-Camp of Napoleon.'"—*New York Mail and Express.*

"'An Aide-de-Camp of Napoleon' is the title of one of the most interesting of the many works which have been published concerning the career of the great warrior."—*New York Press.*

"The memoirs of Count de Ségur are distinguished by all the light graces that can polish a recital and impart delicacy to a narrative without depriving it of its strength. It is a pleasure to peruse this well-written memorial of one who was a general of division, peer of France, and Academician, and who lived for the greater part of a century a brilliant figure in war, politics, and letters."—*Philadelphia Public Ledger.*

"It is not only full of personal reminiscence, but of personal adventure, and, as the style is easy and admirable, neither conceited nor tedious, it is needless to say that the result is exceedingly interesting."—*Boston Commercial Bulletin.*

"The book is a delightful one, not only for its clear, flowing style and historical interest, but for the entire absence of anything approaching bombast or straining for effect. . . . This is one of the most interesting publications that the Napoleonic revival has given us."—*Cleveland World.*

"Next to the memoirs of the private secretary, the Baron de Méneval, issued by the Appletons a year ago, this volume of Ségur's is of greatest interest."—*Rochester Herald.*

New York: D. APPLETON & CO., 72 Fifth Avenue.

D. APPLETON AND COMPANY'S PUBLICATIONS.

*M*EMOIRS OF MARSHAL OUDINOT, Duc de Reggio. Compiled from the hitherto unpublished souvenirs of the Duchesse de Reggio by GASTON STIEGLER, and now first translated into English by Alexander Teixeira de Mattos. With two Portraits in Heliogravure. 12mo. Cloth, $2.00.

"The 'Memoirs of Marshal Oudinot' are interesting because they include the history of one of the most brilliant periods the world has ever seen."—*Chicago Evening Post.*

"The reading of this charming, vivacious, and accurate book makes it a continual source of wonder that any one, at this day, should be writing a history of the Napoleonic era. . . . The complete unconsciousness and the exquisite naturalness of the style are charming."—*New York Commercial Advertiser.*

"This frankly loyal and graphic picturing of a great man's true character, seen from the nearest standpoints by a biographer of wonderful keenness, is genuinely refreshing. Vivid and explicit without being unduly sentimental, it is a book distinctly invaluable to and actually inseparable from a study of French history."—*Boston Globe.*

"It is for the side lights of the marshal's life that this book is chiefly valuable, and wonderfully illuminating they are. Besides, there is a never-ending charm in the freshness of the narrative. There is nothing that is dull or monotonous."—*Chicago Journal.*

"Full of new and entertaining material, and has a really significant historical value. . . . These memoirs are noteworthy for their gentleness of tone and their freedom from satire and vituperation. They deal with great events, and their very simplicity and unpretentiousness are evidence of their incontestable merit."—*Boston Beacon.*

"The story of this gallant soldier is of strong romantic interest and makes excellent reading, while the side lights thrown on events of a long period marked by many extraordinary changes are vastly interesting and informing. It is an inspiring and thoroughly delightful volume."—*Providence News.*

"Few French commanders were more popular, both with rulers and with the people. The eventful story of his life, modestly told, is charming in interest."—*Chicago Inter-Ocean.*

"The pages are filled with illustrious names that arouse pleasant or unpleasant memories, and the reader reads eagerly onward, always entertained, frequently enlightened, until the last page is reached. . . . It will be equally welcomed by the student of history and by the general reader."—*Boston Saturday Evening Gazette.*

"Amid the mass of French memorial writing there is none that will be found more attractive, because there is none more genuine than this record."—*Chicago Times-Herald.*

"An extremely interesting addition to historical biography. . . . These memoirs relate the extraordinary career of an extraordinary man. . . . A complete biography, written in an easy, natural, unpretentious style."—*Detroit Free Press.*

D. APPLETON AND COMPANY, NEW YORK.

D. APPLETON & CO.'S PUBLICATIONS.

*M*EMOIRS ILLUSTRATING THE HISTORY OF NAPOLEON I, *from 1802 to 1815.* By Baron CLAUDE-FRANÇOIS DE MÉNEVAL, Private Secretary to Napoleon. Edited by his Grandson, Baron NAPOLEON JOSEPH DE MÉNEVAL. With Portraits and Autograph Letters. In three volumes. 8vo. Cloth, $6.00.

"The Baron de Méneval knew Napoleon as few knew him. He was his confidential secretary and intimate friend. . . . Students and historians who wish to form a trustworthy estimate of Napoleon can not afford to neglect this testimony by one of his most intimate associates."—*London News.*

"These Memoirs, by the private secretary of Napoleon, are a valuable and important contribution to the history of the Napoleonic period, and necessarily they throw new and interesting light on the personality and real sentiments of the emperor. If Napoleon anywhere took off the mask, it was in the seclusion of his private cabinet. The Memoirs have been republished almost as they were written, by Baron de Méneval's grandson, with the addition of some supplementary documents."—*London Times.*

"Méneval has brought the living Napoleon clearly before us in a portrait, flattering, no doubt, but essentially true to nature; and he has shown us what the emperor really was—at the head of his armies, in his Council of State, as the ruler of France, as the lord of the continent—above all, in the round of his daily life and in the circle of family and home."—*London Academy.*

"Neither the editor nor translator of Méneval's Memoirs has miscalculated his deep interest—an interest which does not depend on literary style but on the substance of what is related. Whoever reads this volume will wait with impatience for the remainder."—*New York Tribune.*

"The work will take rank with the most important of memoirs relating to the period. Its great value arises largely from its author's transparent veracity. Méneval was one of those men who could not consciously tell anything but the truth. He was constitutionally unfitted for lying. . . . The book is extremely interesting, and it is as important as it is interesting."—*New York Times.*

"Few memoirists have given us a more minute account of Napoleon. . . . No lover of Napoleon, no admirer of his wonderful genius, can fail to read these interesting and important volumes which have been waited for for years."—*New York World.*

"The book will be hailed with delight by the collectors of Napoleonic literature, as it covers much ground wholly unexplored by the great majority of the biographers of Napoleon."—*Providence Journal.*

"Méneval made excellent use of the rare opportunity he enjoyed of studying closely and at close range the personality of the supreme genius in human history."—*Philadelphia Press.*

"Of all the memoirs illustrating the history of the first Napoleon—and their number is almost past counting—there is probably not one which will be found of more value to the judicious historian, or of more interest to the general reader than these."—*New York Independent.*

New York: D. APPLETON & CO., 72 Fifth Avenue.

D. APPLETON AND COMPANY'S PUBLICATIONS.

LITERATURES OF THE WORLD. Edited by EDMUND GOSSE, Hon. M. A. of Trinity College, Cambridge.

A succession of attractive volumes dealing with the history of literature in each country. Each volume will contain about three hundred and fifty 12mo pages, and will treat an entire literature, giving a uniform impression of its development, history, and character, and of its relation to previous and to contemporary work.

Each, 12mo, cloth, $1.50.

NOW READY.

ANCIENT GREEK LITERATURE. By GILBERT MURRAY, M. A., Professor of Greek in the University of Glasgow.

"Mr. Murray has produced a book which fairly represents the best conclusions of modern scholarship with regard to the Greeks."—*London Times.*

FRENCH LITERATURE. By EDWARD DOWDEN, D. C. L., LL. D., Professor of English Literature at the University of Dublin.

"Certainly the best history of French literature in the English language."—*London Athenæum.*

MODERN ENGLISH LITERATURE. By the EDITOR.

The aim of this informing and well-balanced volume is to show the movement of English literature, and to give the reader a feeling of its evolution, the slow unwinding of the threads of literary expression down succeeding generations. The author has retained the character of a historical survey with the introduction of the obvious names, but he has kept before him expression, form, and technique as the central interest.

IN PREPARATION.

AMERICAN.

ITALIAN. By RICHARD GARNETT, C. B., LL. D., Keeper of Printed Books in the British Museum.

GERMAN. By Dr. C. H. HERFORD, Professor of English Literature in the University of Wales.

HUNGARIAN. By Dr. ZOLTÁN BEÖTHY, Professor of Hungarian Literature at the University of Budapest.

LATIN. By Dr. ARTHUR WOOLGAR VERRALL, Fellow and Senior Tutor of Trinity College, Cambridge.

JAPANESE. By W. G. ASTON, C. M. G., M. A., late Acting Secretary at the British Legation at Tokio.

MODERN SCANDINAVIAN. By Dr. GEORG BRANDES, of Copenhagen.

SPANISH. By J. FITZ MAURICE-KELLY, Member of the Spanish Academy.

SANSCRIT. By A. A MACDONELL, M. A., Deputy Boden Professor of Sanscrit at the University of Oxford.

D. APPLETON AND COMPANY, NEW YORK.

D. APPLETON AND COMPANY'S PUBLICATIONS.

THE ANTHROPOLOGICAL SERIES.

NOW READY.

THE BEGINNINGS OF ART. By ERNST GROSSE, Professor of Philosophy in the University of Freiburg. A new volume in the Anthropological Series, edited by Professor Frederick Starr. Illustrated. 12mo. Cloth, $1.75.

"This book can not fail to interest students of every branch of art, while the general reader who will dare to take hold of it will have his mind broadened and enriched beyond what he would conceive a work of many times its dimensions might effect."—*Brooklyn Eagle.*

WOMAN'S SHARE IN PRIMITIVE CULTURE. By OTIS TUFTON MASON, A. M., Curator of the Department of Ethnology in the United States National Museum. With numerous Illustrations. 12mo. Cloth, $1.75.

"A most interesting *résumé* of the revelations which science has made concerning the habits of human beings in primitive times, and especially as to the place, the duties, and the customs of women."—*Philadelphia Inquirer.*

THE PYGMIES. By A. DE QUATREFAGES, late Professor of Anthropology at the Museum of Natural History, Paris. With numerous Illustrations. 12mo. Cloth, $1.75.

"This book ought to be in every divinity school in which man as well as God is studied, and from which missionaries go out to convert the human being of reality and not the man of rhetoric and text-books."—*Boston Literary World.*

THE BEGINNINGS OF WRITING. By W. J. HOFFMAN, M. D. With numerous Illustrations. 12mo. Cloth, $1.75.

This interesting book gives a most attractive account of the rude methods employed by primitive man for recording his deeds. The earliest writing consists of pictographs which were traced on stone, wood, bone, skins, and various paperlike substances. Dr. Hoffman shows how the several classes of symbols used in these records are to be interpreted, and traces the growth of conventional signs up to syllabaries and alphabets—the two classes of signs employed by modern peoples.

IN PREPARATION.

THE SOUTH SEA ISLANDERS. By Dr. SCHMELTZ.
THE ZUÑI. By FRANK HAMILTON CUSHING.
THE AZTECS. By Mrs. ZELIA NUTTALL.

D. APPLETON AND COMPANY, NEW YORK.

www.ingramcontent.com/pod-product-compliance
Lightning Source LLC
Chambersburg PA
CBHW030255170426
43202CB00009B/754